100 MICRO CROCHET MOTIFS

Patterns and charts for tiny crochet creations

Steffi Glaves

DAVID & CHARLES

www.davidandcharles.com

Contents

Welcome

Tiny objects are fascinating. From dollhouse miniatures and model railways, to jewellery charms and tiny food, anything that can shrink to fit in the palm of your hand can instantly become more precious with new possibilities for different applications. The same can be said for crochet, the classic granny square transforms into something unique and special when reduced to the size of a postage stamp.

This book, 100 Micro-Crochet Motifs, demonstrates how to do just that with your own crochet. With 10 themed chapters and a fun project for each one, there is a wide range of tiny and beautiful crochet pieces that can be used in so many ways.

You will learn the central skills needed for micro-crochet, such as how to hold the thread and hook, reading a crochet chart, special edgings, blocking and stiffening. Alongside that, you will also learn about the tools and types of threads to use, and the special techniques needed for creating the motifs in this book, such as incorporating wire, creating tiny keepsake bags and making your own jewellery. There are simple motifs with 2 to 4 rounds of crochet and more challenging ones with more rounds, colour changes and different stitches – some of them are 3D amigurumi.

These motifs are not just for micro-crochet: scale them up with standard DK yarn and a larger crochet hook for bigger motifs which have their own charm, and use them for bunting and bouquets. The envelope project in the Blanket Squares chapter is a great example of this as it involves using the same granny square design to make a miniscule pendant or a larger belt purse.

This book is for anyone who already has a grasp of the basic crochet stitches and techniques, and wishes to explore making jewellery, accessories, appliqués, or just tiny things for the sheer joy of it.

Before you begin

Before diving into the motifs, refer to this section for guidance on threads, hooks and tips and tricks on working micro-crochet. The motifs are split into 10 themed chapters with a fun project for each one. Also have a look at the Techniques section for how to incorporate other techniques such as blocking and jewellery making.

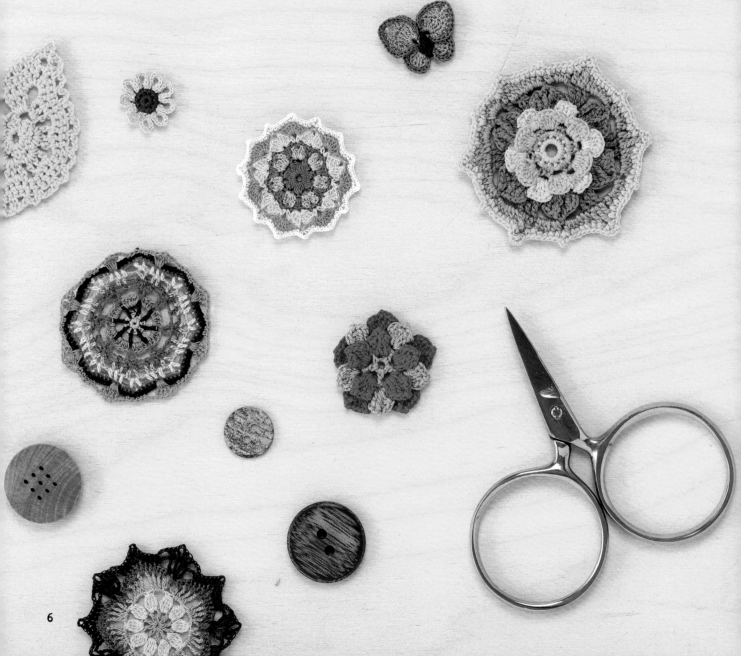

TOOLS AND MATERIALS

Let's start by looking at the threads and yarns used in this book.

There are lots of different types of thread that are suitable for micro-crochet, varying in thickness and application, so you can slowly transition from crochet using standard yarns and hooks to using finer threads and hooks.

Here are the main things to look out for when purchasing your own threads.

Thickness/gauge number

Threads specifically made for fine crochet have a number to indicate the thickness or gauge. The higher the number, the finer the thread. Most common gauges are 10, 20, 30, 40, 50, 60, 70, 80 and 100. I use sewing cotton more than crochet cotton and use the equivalent of gauge 80 with a 0.5mm (12 steel) hook for most of my work. Common sewing threads will not have this numbering system.

Mercerised

You will often see this on packaging for crochet threads. Mercerised cotton means that it has undergone a chemical and heat process to give it a lustre.

'Fibre halo' is particularly important if you are looking at sewing threads. Put a thread strand up to the light – do you see a halo of fibres around the main core of the thread? Most threads will have this, but too much will reduce the appearance of definition in the stitches of your work and make it prone to tangling.

Strength

Even the finest of threads can be strong. If it snaps easily, then I wouldn't recommend crocheting with it. There is nothing worse than achieving the perfect magic ring, only for the tail end to snap off as you are drawing it to a close! This will not usually happen with specific crochet threads but there is a risk with sewing threads.

Colour range

When looking at different ranges and brands of threads consider the following – does this brand have a range of colours that appeal to you? Can these threads be combined easily with others you have at home? There is nothing wrong with combining thread brands, though major differences in thread thickness may affect the overall look of your crochet pieces.

Reduce thread weight and crochet hook size gradually to get used to working at a micro scale.

Thread classification

EMBROIDERY THREADS

These are great threads to start with as they are cheap, available in many colours, may often be in your existing craft stash and they can be stranded down to desired thicknesses. Pearl (or perlé) cotton can also be used for embroidery and crochet. It has a subtle sheen and silky feel.

GÜTERMANN TOP STITCHING THREAD

This is a polyester thread which is great for trying out micro-crochet for the first time. It's proper purpose is for strong stitching on heavy duty fabrics such as denim. It is readily available in shops and is low in cost.

The hooks I use for this type of thread are a 0.75mm (14/10 steel) hook especially for amigurumi but a 0.9mm-1mm (14/8 to **12/6** steel) can also be used.

GÜTERMANN HAND QUILTING COTTON

This is a very lightly waxed cotton which gives fantastic definition to the stitches and a little more strength. It is smooth, with a subtle sheen and low friction properties, which makes it great for tiny magic rings and it can be repeatedly frogged.

Though it is slightly expensive for 200m, a little goes a long way, and the threads are wound on a spool which have a hidden compartment for needles, making it suitable for travel without tangling.

The colour range is limited, compared to specialised crochet cottons, but it is more readily available in local haberdasheries. Do note that this thread is not suitable for sewing machine use.

I use a 0.5mm (12 steel) hook, but a 0.6mm (12 steel) hook can also be used.

CONNECTING THREADS QUILTING COTTON

This is an American brand and they have a wide range of colours that are available to order from their website. They are good value for money as they consist of 1200m per spool. They are great for making tassels and incorporating them into jewellery.

I use a 0.5mm (12 steel) hook for these threads.

DMC

DMC has the widest range of crochet cottons and gauges, useful for those who want to gradually go down the threads and hook sizes.

Special Dentelles 80 is a fine 3-ply lace-making crochet cotton that has been combed, singed by flame and twice mercerised. There are 72 colours to choose from with lots of bright as well as subtle shades, together with a small range of colour gradients that change from white to a colour. They are wound on adorable little balls but they can unravel easily so I recommend storing them with bands or in individual bags. They are good value for money, but not so common in local crafts shop. They can, however, be ordered directly from the DMC website.

I use a 0.5mm (12 steel) hook, but a 0.6mm (12 steel) hook can also be used. Special Dentelles can be combined with Gütermann hand quilting cotton.

Other ranges by DMC include **Cabeblia**, which is available in 31 colours in gauges 10 to 40.

Cardonnet is available in gauges 10 to 80 but is limited to white shades. This is a good range to look at if you are interested in dying the threads after crocheting.

DMC also have thicker crochet yarns available such as **Petra**, which is suitable for 1.5mm (8/7/2 steel) to 3.5mm (00) hooks.

There are other fantastic brands such as **Coats and Anchor**. A lot of the threads are intended for lacy clothing and baby clothing, so they are often available online in large quantities.

Crochet hooks

Now let's move onto crochet hooks. There are a couple of things to bear in mind when choosing these.

HOOK SIZE VARIATIONS

You can choose a hook different to the one recommended. When working at a minute scale, where differences in hook sizes can be 0.1mm, there can be subtle differences from brand to brand. They can also slightly differ in hook shape and curve, so it is important to consider different ones. For example, I use a 0.5mm (12 steel) hook for gauge 80 crochet cotton as I have quite tight tension – you may prefer a 0.6mm (12 steel) hook.

HANDLES AND BRANDS

Some hooks are available with or without handles. I certainly recommend buying one with a handle for comfort. They come in different sizes, materials, shapes and textures. I use a **Clover Soft Touch**, which is flat with a grip pad. Clover also has the **Amour Soft Grip** range that has a rounder handle with a silicone grip. Another good brand is **Tulip** which offers **Etimo Steel** and **Etimo Rose** for a more ergonomic grip.

AVAILABILITY

It is always preferable to have a look at the hook in store rather than buying online, however, micro-crochet is not as commonly practised as regular crochet, so very small hooks are not always on the shelves in your local craft shop. If they stock brands such as Clover and Tulip, it is always worth asking if one can be ordered in for you – that is how I got my first micro-crochet hook!

The table shown here lists which hooks I use for which thread gauges. I have a tight tension, which is ideal for micro-crochet, so I prefer a finer hook. There is flexibility in going up or down a size depending on your preferred tension. If you feel that your tension is too tight, I recommend going up a hook size, like you would with regular crochet.

Thread	UK Hook	US Hook
3	1.75 to 2mm (DMC recommends 3.5mm)	4/0 to 4 steel
5	1.25 to 1.5mm (DMC recommends 2.5mm)	9/4 to 8/7/2 steel
8	0.9mm to 1mm (DMC recommends 1.5mm)	14/8 to 12/6 steel
10	0.9mm to 1mm	14/8 to 12/6 steel
20	0.9mm	14/8 steel
30	0.9mm	14/8 steel
40	0.75mm to 0.9mm	14/10 to 14/8 steel
50	0.75mm	14/10 steel
60	0.75mm	14/10 steel
70	0.6mm	12 steel
80	0.5mm to 0.6mm	12 steel
Sewing threads	0.35 to 0.5mm	12 steel

Other items

Items which come in handy include sewing needles, rubber thimbles, jewellery findings, pliers, bulldog clips, sandpaper, stiffening materials and stuffing materials. For further information on the use of these see the Techniques section.

Danish heart mini pendant

Envelope necklace

Clam shell pendant

Meadow embroidery hoop

Project gallery

A handy visual guide to all of the beautiful miniature projects you'll find in this book.

Envelope belt purse

Flower jewellery

Framed mandala

Amigurumi cake slice

Mis-matched planet earrings

Ivy strand bracelet

Cake topper

Flowers

These tiny flowers are ideal for jewellery and appliqués. Team them with motifs from the leaf chapter for beautiful customisable arrangements. All use Gütermann hand quilting cotton with 0.5mm or 0.6mm (12 steel) hook.

FORGET-ME-NOT/CHERRY BLOSSOM

Materials

- 0.5mm-0.6mm (12 steel) crochet hook
- Embroidery needle

Finished size

12mm x 12mm (½in x ½in)

Forget-Me-Not

- Gütermann hand quilting cotton, colours used in this order: Yellow 758, Mid Blue 5725; **For embroidery**: White 5709

Cherry Blossom

- Gütermann hand quilting cotton, colours used in this order: Dark Red 2833, Light Pink 2538; **For embroidery**: Dusky Pink 2635

Round 1: Make a magic ring, 10dc into ring, ss in first dc to finish (10 sts).

Round 2: Change colour, ss in any st, *(3ch, 1tr) in same dc, 1ch, (1tr, 3ch, ss) in next dc, ss in next dc, rep from * 4 times, ending with ss in first dc.

Round 3: *4dc into next 3ch sp, (1dc, 2ch, 1dc) in next 1ch sp, 4dc in 3ch sp, ss in round 1 dc, ss into next round 1 dc, rep from * 4 times, ending with ss in first round 1 dc to finish.

To embroider the little V shapes between the petals, double up the thread and sew from between each petal into the dc sts of round 1. Sew in and trim ends.

SUNFLOWER/DAISY

Materials

- 0.5mm-0.6mm (12 steel) crochet hook
- Embroidery needle

Finished size

15mm x 15mm (⅝in x ⅝in)

Sunflower

- Gütermann hand quilting cotton, colours used in this order: Brown 1833, Yellow 758

Daisy

- Gütermann hand quilting cotton, colours used in this order: Yellow 758, White 5709

Round 1: Make a magic ring, 9dc into ring, ss in first dc to finish (9 sts).

Round 2: 2dc in each st to end, ss in first dc (18 sts).

Round 3: Change colour, work over the thread end from round 2 as you go to weave in, ss in any st, *(ss, 6ch, ss) into next st, ss in next st, rep from * 8 times, ending with ss in same place as beg ss.

Round 4: *ss in round 2 st at base of petal, (1ch, 4dc, 2ch, 4dc, 1ch) in 6ch sp, ss in same st, skip next st from round 2, rep from * 8 times, ss in same place as beg ss to finish.

Sew in and trim ends.

ORCHID

Materials

- 0.5mm-0.6mm (12 steel) crochet hook
- Gütermann hand quilting cotton, colours used in this order: Light Ivory 919, Light Pink 2538, Light Ivory 919 (again), Yellow 758
- Bead embroidery needle
- 2mm bead

Finished size

20mm x 18mm (¾in x ¾in)

Layer 1

Round 1: Make a magic ring, 9dc into ring, close ring but do not ss to finish (9 sts).

Round 2: *(Ss, 6ch, 3ttr, 6ch, ss) in beg st, ss in next 2 sts, rep from * twice.

Round 3: *Ss in next round 1 st, 1ch, (3dc, 5htr) in 6ch sp, 2tr in next sp between sts, 1ch, 2tr in next sp between sts, (5htr, 3dc) in 6ch sp, 1ch, ss in same round 1 st, 2ch to reach next petal base st, rep from * twice, ss in first dc.

Round 4: *Ss into round 1 st at base of petal, (1ch, ss) in every st and ch sp around petal, ss into round 1 st at base of petal, 2ch to reach next round 1 base petal st, rep from * twice, ss in first dc.

Layer 2

Round 1: Using Pink make a magic ring, 12dc into ring, ss in first dc to finish, leave long excess thread for sewing.

Round 2: Using Ivory (ss, 4ch, 3dtr, 4ch, ss) in any st.

Round 3: 2ch, turn, 6htr in 4ch sp, 2tr in next sp between sts, 1ch, 2tr in next sp between sts, 6htr in 4ch sp, 2ch, ss in same round 1 st at base of petal.

Round 4: 2ch, turn, starting first htr st (ss, 1ch) in every st and ch sp around petal, 2ch after last htr, ss in round 1 st at base of petal. Do not turn.

4ch, skip 4 sts from round 1, rep rounds 2 to 4 in the next st to make second petal.

Round 5: Using Yellow, starting at the third st from the left hand petal, (ss, 2ch, 1tr, 2ch, ss) in the next 2 sts.

Trim and fasten ends. Use excess thread from layer 2 round 1 to sew bead into magic ring and sew to layer 1.

PANSY

Materials

- 0.5mm-0.6mm (12 steel) crochet hook
- Gütermann hand quilting cotton, colours used in this order: Dark Purple 3832, Lilac 4434; **For embroidery**: White 5709, Yellow 758
- Embroidery needle

Finished size

10mm x 10mm (⅜in x ⅜in)

Round 1: Make a magic ring, (4ch, 4tr, 4ch, ss) in ring, *(3ch, 2tr, 3ch, ss) in ring, rep from * once, pull ring to a close loosely, 4ch, move these ch sts to behind the petals, ss on opposite side of petals, between bottom and top petal to secure ch. Put thread to one side but do not trim it.

Round 2: Change colour, ss in magic ring, between bottom and top right petal, *3dc in 3ch sp, 2dc between 2 tr sts, 3dc in ch sp, ss in magic ring, rep petal, rep from * for second top petal, (3dc, 1htr) in 4ch sp of bottom petal, 1htr in each of the 3 sps between next 4 htr, (1htr, 3dc) in 4ch sp, ss in magic ring.

Row 3: 1ch, ss in 4ch sp behind petals, [4ch, 2dtr, 4ch, ss in ch sp] twice.

Row 4: Turn, [3ch, 2dc in petal 4ch sp, 2dc between dtr sts, 2dc in next 4ch sp, 3ch, ss in base ch sp] twice, ss in base ch sp to finish, trim and sew in ends.

Row 5: Pick up the dark purple thread, ss in base ch cp, [2ch, 1dc in ch sp, 1dc in next st, 2dc in next st, 1dc in next 2 sts, 2dc in next st, 1dc in next st, 1dc in ch sp, 2ch, ss in base ch sp] twice to finish.

Using White sew 2 sts from the magic ring to between the 2tr sts of the top petals, sewing through the back petals at the same time to keep them in position.

Using Yellow sew 3 sts from the magic ring to between the tr sps of the bottom petal in round 1.

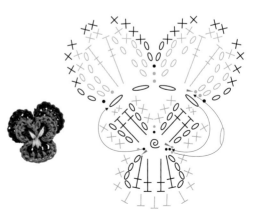

LOBELIA

Materials

- 0.5mm-0.6mm (12 steel) crochet hook
- Gütermann hand quilting cotton in Lilac 4434; **For embroidery:** White 5709
- Embroidery needle

Finished size

20mm x 16mm (¾in x ⅝in)

Round 1: Make a magic ring, 1ch (does not count as dc), 5dc, 1htr, 1tr, 3ch, 1tr, 1htr, pull magic ring to close but do not join round.

Round 2: (Ss, 6ch, 1ttr, 6ch, ss) in beg st of round 1, ss in next st, *(ss, 6ch, 1ttr, 6ch, ss) in next st of round 1, ss in next st, rep from * once, (ss, 3ch, ss) in next st, 2ch, (2tr, 3ch picot, 1tr) in 3ch sp, 2ch, (ss, 3ch, ss) in next st, ss in next st.

Round 3: Ss in round 1 st at base of first petal, (3dc, 5tr) in 6ch sp, 3tr in ttr, (1dc, 3tr, 3dc) in next 6ch sp, ss in round 1 st at base of petal, ss in next 2 round 1 sts, (3dc, 1htr, 3tr, 1dc) in next 6ch sp, 3htr in ttr, (1dc, 3tr, 1htr, 1dc) in next 6ch sp, ss in round 1 st at base of petal, ss in next 2 round 1 sts, (3dc, 3tr, 1dc) in 6ch sp, 3tr in ttr, (5tr, 3dc) in last 6ch sp, ss in round 1 st at base of petal, trim and sew in ends.

Using White embroider the centre, working stitches from the magic ring to between the petals.

POPPY

Materials

- 0.5mm-0.6mm (12 steel) crochet hook
- Gütermann hand quilting cotton, colours used in this order: Black 5201, Red 2453
- Embroidery needle

Finished size

10mm x 10mm (⅜in x ⅜in)

Round 1: Make a magic ring, 8dc into ring, ss in first dc to finish (8 sts).

Round 2: Change colour, *ss in first dc st from round 1, (3ch, 3tr) in same st, 2tr in next 2 sts, (3tr, 3ch, ss) in next st, rep from * starting with a ss in the next dc.

Round 3: *ss in first dc from round 1, 1ch, 4dc into 3ch sp, 2dc between each of next 10 tr (9 pairs of dc), 4dc in next 3ch sp, 1ch, ss in fourth st from round 1, rep from * to finish, starting with a ss in the next dc.

PINK PERENNIAL

Materials

- 0.5mm-0.6mm (12 steel) crochet hook
- Gütermann hand quilting cotton in Bright Pink 2955
- Embroidery needle

Finished size

8mm x 8mm (¼in x ¼in)

This pattern is a great introduction to crochet flowers, because it is one round which can be worked in a magic ring or an 8ch circle. The centre has a hole, great for sewing in a seed bead for decoration.

You will notice one side of the petals has one less chain stitch than the other. This is to maintain definition to the individual petals when working at this scale. If this doesn't suit you and your tension, make 2 chain stitches on each side.

Round 1: Make a magic ring or 8ch, [2ch, 5tr, 1ch, ss] 5 times in magic ring, close magic ring and use excess thread to sew a bead in the centre.

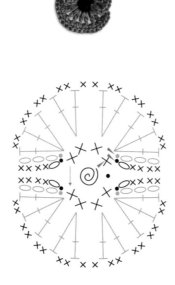

SENTIMENTAL BLUE

Materials

- 0.5mm-0.6mm (12 steel) crochet hook
- Gütermann hand quilting cotton in Turquoise 6934
- Bead embroidery needle
- 2mm bead

Finished size

18mm x 18mm (¾in x ¾in)

Round 1: Make a magic ring, 15dc into ring, ss in first dc (15 sts).

Round 2: ss in first dc, *4ch, skip 2 dc, ss in next dc, rep from * 4 times ending with ss in beg dc.

Round 3: (ss, 4ch, 2dtr, 4ch, ss) in every 5ch sp.

Round 4: *ss in round 2 ch sp, 1ch, 4dc in 4ch sp, (dc, 2ch, dc) between dtr sts, 4dc in 4ch sp, 1ch, ss in same round 2 ch sp, rep from * 4 times.

Round 5: *ss in round 2 ch sp, 1ch, 1dc in next 3 sts, 2dc in next st, 1dc in next st, (1dc, 2ch, 1dc) in 2ch sp, 1dc in next st, 2dc in next st, 1dc in rem 3 dc sts of petal, 1ch, ss in same round 2 ch sp, rep from * 4 times

Sew the bead into the centre of the magic ring.

VINCA CIRCLE

Materials

- 0.5mm-0.6mm (12 steel) crochet hook
- Gütermann hand quilting cotton, colours used in this order: Dusky Teal 7325, Turquoise 6934, Light Ivory 919, Royal Blue 5133
- Embroidery needle

Finished size

12mm x 12mm (½in x ½in)

Round 1: Make a magic ring, [2dc, 2ch] 5 times into ring, ss in first dc to finish.

Round 2: Change colour, ss in any 2ch sp, 3ch (counts as 1tr), 4tr in same sp, 5tr in each of next 5 sps, invisible ss (see Techniques: Special Stitches) or regular ss in beg tr to finish.

Round 3: Change colour, starting in third (centre) tr of shell st, 1dc in next 3 sts, *1dc between the shell sts and between 2 dc sts of round 2, drawing up a long thread before last yarn-over-pull-through to prevent puckering, 1dc in next 5 sts, rep from * 3 times, 1dc between the shell sts and between 2 dc sts of round 2, drawing up a long thread before last yarn-over-pull-through to prevent puckering, 1dc in next 2 sts, invisible ss in beg dc to finish.

Round 4: Change colour, ss in second st of round 3, 1back-dc (crab st) in every st, 1back-dc over beg ss, ss in next st to the right.

Sew in and trim ends.

FOLDED CLEMATIS

Materials

- 0.5mm-0.6mm (12 steel) crochet hook
- Gütermann hand quilting cotton, colours used in this order: Dark Red 2833, Pink 3526
- Embroidery needle

Finished size

15mm x 15mm (⅝in x ⅝in)

Round 1: Make a magic ring, 12dc into ring, ss in first dc to finish.

Round 2: Change colour, 6ch (counts as 1tr, 3ch), *1tr, 3ch, skip 1 st, rep from * 3 times, ss in third ch of 6ch.

Round 3: *4ch, ss in next tr st, 2ch, turn, (5tr, 2ch, 2tr) in round 2 and 3 ch sps together, 7dtr around post of tr directly below, ss in next tr st to fold sts over (see chart, makes one folded petal), rep from * 5 times to finish.

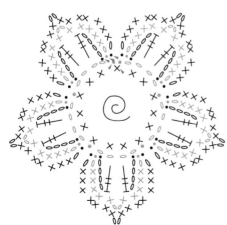

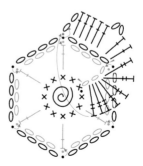

Flower jewellery

This project shows how to transform
flower motifs into wearable jewellery
pieces by attaching a crocheted
disc to neaten the backs and adding
jewellery findings. Mix-and-match the
different motifs and make them look
like a set by changing the colours.
The Sentimental Blue flower looks
more like a hellebore when crocheted
in green and teams well with the
Forget-Me-Not earrings.

Materials

- 0.5mm-0.6mm (12 steel) crochet hook
- Gütermann hand quilting cotton in colours
  of your choice. I used Dusky Pink 2635, Light
  Green 7918, Dusky Teal 7325
- For pendant: medium split bail or 1 jump ring
  large enough to fit a chain through
- For earrings: 4 small jump rings, 3mm in
  diameter, 2 ear wires
- Needle nose jewellery pliers
- Scissors
- Bead embroidery needle

Finished size

As per chosen flowers

Crochet the flower of your choice and a backing disc to cover the sewn in ends at the back. Disc sizes can differ depending on the flower, however the rule of thumb is that it needs to have at least two rounds of crochet. The finished disc needs to be slightly smaller than the base of the petals and the number of stitches in the last round needs to be a multiple of the number of petals. Use the smaller chart for the Forget-Me-Not and the larger chart for the Sentimental Blue.

Crochet the backing discs

Forget-Me-Not has 5 petals, 2 rounds, 3 sts per petal = 15 sts on last round.

Round 1: Make a magic ring, into ring work 10dc, ss in first dc.

Round 2: (1dc, 2dc in next st) to end, makes 15 sts, ss in first dc, leave long length of thread for sewing.

Sentimental Blue Flower has 5 petals but is bigger, so 2 rounds, 4 sts per petal = 20 sts on last round.

Round 1: Make a magic ring, into ring work 10dc, ss in first dc.

Round 2: 2dc in every st, makes 20 sts.

Round 3: 1dc in every st, ss to first dc, leave long length of thread for sewing.

Necklace: position your backing disc so that the end of round and excess thread is in the 11 o'clock position. Use a crochet hook to prise a larger hole just below the magic ring **(1)**.

Open the split bail and thread the narrow end through the prised hole. Close in place using pliers, covering the magic ring to make sure it is straight. Try not to flatten the top of the bail in the process, you need it rounded and open so that a chain can fit through **(2)**.

Position the backing disc onto the back of the flower so that the bail sits centrally behind a petal or between two petals, depending on your preference **(3 and 4)**.

Use excess thread to whip stitch the back loops of the backing disc to the base of the petals. Sew 3 stitches to the petal on either side of the bail and 4 stitches to each remaining petal. Being methodical like this ensures the backing disc is secured and the bail won't change position while you sew **(5)**.

Earrings: crochet a backing disc and use the excess thread to stitch the back loops to the base of the petals. Prise open a 2-chain space or stitch on the flower motif with a crochet hook, thread an opened jump ring through and close with pliers. For small earrings, you will need to attach another small jump ring and an ear wire **(6)**.

Leaves

The leaves in this chapter are ideal to make
when you can't decide between spring and autumn
projects. Combine them with motifs from the flower
chapter for a tiny bouquet or work single pieces
for jewellery. You could crochet the same pattern
in different colours, or go for mis-matched
earrings. Another option using DK yarn is to make
autumnal bunting for Thanksgiving home décor.

FOUR LEAF CLOVER

Materials

- 0.5mm-0.6mm (12 steel) crochet hook
- Gütermann hand quilting cotton in Emerald Green 8244
- Embroidery needle
- Glue or clear nail varnish (optional)

Finished size

16mm x 20mm (⅝in x ¾in)

Round 1: Make a magic ring, *4dc into ring, (5ch, 2trtr, 5ch, ss) in last dc made, (makes leaf), rep from * 3 times, 2dc, ss in beg dc.

Round 2: *ss in next 3 sts, ss into dc at base of leaf, (3dc, 1htr, 5tr, 1htr) in 5ch sp, ss between 2 trtr sts, (1htr, 5tr, 1htr, 3dc) in 5ch sp, ss into same dc st at base of leaf, rep from * 3 times.

Stalk: ss in next 2 dc so that the stalk starts evenly between the 2 bottom leaves, (3ch, 1tr) into same dc (makes loop), (3ch, 1tr) into loop sp (makes second loop), continue making loops in this way until desired length is achieved, ss in last st.

Trim and sew in ends. Alternatively, add a tiny dab of glue or clear nail varnish to the end of the stalk. Allow to dry thoroughly before trimming.

OAK LEAF

Materials

- 0.75mm-1mm (14/10-12/6 steel) crochet hook
- Gütermann top stitching thread in Fox Orange 982
- Embroidery needle

Finished size

20mm x 35mm (¾in x 1⅜in)

Round 1: Make a magic ring, 3ch, 1tr into ring (makes loop), *3ch, 1tr in loop sp, (makes second loop), rep from * until a string of 5 loop sps are made.

Round 2: 3dc in top loop sp, 3htr in next loop sp, 3tr in next loop sp, 3dtr in next loop sp, 13dtr in bottom loop sp, working up other side of leaf, 3dtr in next loop sp, 3tr in next loop sp, 3htr in next loop sp, 3dc in top loop sp, 6ch, ss in beg dc.

Round 3: ss, 1dc, 2tr in next st, 3tr in next st, 1ch (makes leaf bump), ss in same st, *ss in next 2 sts, 1dc, 1htr, (5tr, 2ch, ss) in next st, rep from * once, ss in next 2 sts, 1ch, 3tr in next st, 3dtr in next st (makes leaf point), 3tr in next st, 1ch, **ss in next 3 sts, 2ch, 5tr in next st, 1htr, 1dc, rep from ** once, ss in next 3 sts, 1ch, 3tr in next st, 2tr in next st, 1dc, ss in next 2 sts, (3dc, 4ch, 3dc) in 6ch sp leaf point, ss in beg dc st.

Trim and sew in ends.

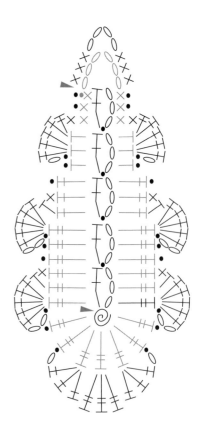

STANDARD LEAF

Materials

- 0.75mm-1mm (14/10-12/6 steel) crochet hook
- Gütermann top stitching thread in Green 235
- Embroidery needle

Finished size

17mm x 37mm (⅝in x 1⅜in)

Round 1: Make a magic ring, (3ch, 1tr) into ring (makes loop), *(3ch, 1tr) in loop sp, (makes second loop), rep from * until a string of 5 loop sps are made.

Round 2: 3ch, 3tr in first loop, *4dtr in next loop, 4ttr in next loop, 4dtr in next loop, 4tr in end loop (makes half a leaf)**, 7ch (for leaf point), 4tr in end loop on the other side, rep from * to ** to make the other side of the leaf, 4ch, 1dtr in beg 3ch sp to make second leaf point.

Round 3: 4dc in dtr sp, 1dc between each pair of sts down side of leaf to leaf point (23dc so far), (4dc, 3ch, 4dc) in leaf point ch sp, 1dc between each pair of sts up other side of leaf, 4dc in leaf point ch sp (54 dc), 2ch, 1tr in beg dc to make leaf point.

Trim and sew in ends.

GRANNY LEAF

Materials

- 0.75mm-1mm (14/10-12/6 steel) crochet hook
- Gütermann top stitching thread in Orange 350
- Embroidery needle

Finished size

23mm x 35mm (⅞in x 1⅜in)

Row 1: Make a magic ring, 3ch (counts as tr), 2tr, 3ch, 3tr all into ring.

Row 2: 4ch, turn work, (4tr, 4ch, 4tr) in centre 3ch sp, 1dtr in beg 3ch sp from row 1.

Row 3: 5ch, turn work, (5dtr, 3ch, 5dtr) in centre 4ch sp, 1ttr in beg 4ch sp from row 2.

Row 4: 5ch, turn work, (4tr, 3ch, 4tr) in centre 3ch sp, 1ttr in beg 5ch sp from row 3.

Row 5: 4ch, turn work, (3tr, 3ch, 3tr) in centre 3ch sp, 1ttr in beg 5ch sp from row 4.

Round 6: *3dc in ttr sp from round 4, (3ch, ss) in last dc worked (makes picot), 2dc in same ttr sp**, rep from * in next 3 st sps, 3dc around outer tr from row 1, (1dc, 4ch, 1dc) in magic ring, 3dc in beg 3ch sp from row 1, rep from * to ** in next 4 st sps up other side of leaf, 1dc between each of next 3 tr, (1dc, 2ch, 1dc) in top 3ch sp, 1dc between each of next 3 tr, ss in beg dc.

Trim and sew in ends.

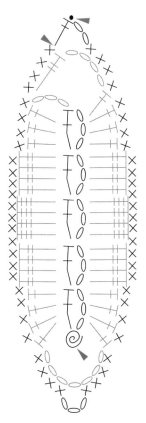

EYE LEAF

Materials

- 0.75mm-1mm (14/10-12/6 steel) crochet hook
- Gütermann top stitching thread, colours used in this order: Green 235, Light Green 152, Fawn 722, Orange 350, Fox Orange 982
- Embroidery needle

Finished size

20mm x 37mm (¾in x 1⅜in)

Round 1: Make a magic ring, 12dc into ring, ss in beg dc to finish.

Round 2: Change colour, 4ch (counts as 1ttr), 1ttr in same dc, 2dtr in next dc, 3tr in each of next 2 dc, 2dtr in next dc, 2ttr in next dc, 4ch (makes leaf point), 2ttr in next dc, 2dtr in next dc, 3tr in each of next 2 dc, 2dtr in next dc, 2ttr in next dc, 2ch, 1tr in 4ch sp for leaf point to finish.

Round 3: Change colour, 2dc in leaf point, 1dc between each of the sts until leaf point is reached (15dc so far), (2dc, 4ch, 2dc) in leaf point, 1dc between all sts on other side of leaf (32dc so far) 2dc in leaf point, 2ch, 1tr in 1st dc to make leaf point and finish.

Round 4: Change colour, 2dc in leaf point sp, 1dc in each st down side of leaf, (2dc, 3ch, 2dc) in bottom leaf point sp, 1dc in each st on other side of leaf, 2dc in beg leaf point sp, 1ch, 1tr in beg dc to finish.

Round 5: Change colour, turn work over, 1dc in leaf point ch sp, turn work back over, work 1back-dc (crab st) in each st down right side of leaf to the leaf point ch sp, turn work over, (1dc, 4ch, 1dc) in leaf ch sp, turn work back over, work 1back-dc in each st up other side of leaf to beg leaf point, turn work over, 1dc in leaf point sp, 4ch, ss in beg dc to finish.

Trim and sew in ends.

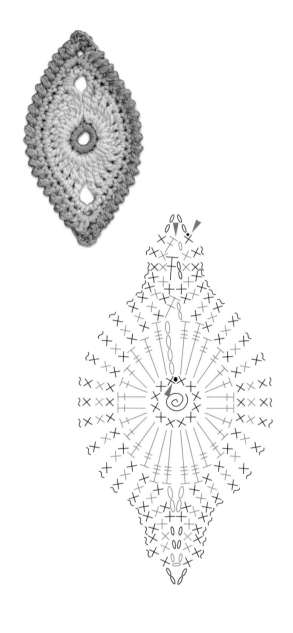

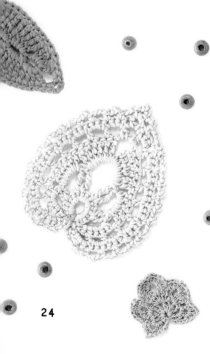

HEART LEAF

Materials

Larger Leaf

- 0.75mm-1mm (14/10-12/6 steel) crochet hook
- Gütermann top stitching thread in Fawn 722
- Embroidery needle

Finished size

32mm x 35mm (1¼in x 1⅜in)

Smaller Leaf

- 0.6mm (12 steel) crochet hook
- Gütermann hand quilting cotton in Mid Green 8724
- Embroidery needle

Finished size

25mm x 29mm (1in x 1⅛in)

Round 1: Make a magic ring, 16dc into ring, ss in beg dc.

Round 2: turn work over, 5ch, skip 1 dc, 2tr in next dc, 4ch, skip 2 dc, 2dtr in next dc, 8ch, skip 2 dc, 2dtr in next dc, 4ch, skip 2 dc, 2tr in next dc, 5ch, skip 1 dc, ss in next dc.

Round 3: turn work over and crochet in the sps not the sts, 1ch, 5dc in first ch sp, 1ch, 6tr in next ch sp, (6dtr, 3ch, 6dtr) in next ch sp, 6tr in next ch sp, 1ch, 5dc in last ch sp, 1ch, ss in beg dc from round 1.

Round 4: turn work over, 3ch, skip 1ch sp, [skip 1 dc, 1htr in next dc, 2ch] twice, skip 1 dc, 1htr in 1ch sp, [2ch, skip 1 st, 1htr in next st] 6 times, (2ch, 1tr, 3ch, 1tr) in leaf point ch sp, 2ch, 1htr in first dtr, [2ch, skip 1 st, 1htr in next st] 5 times up the other side of leaf, 2ch, skip 1 st, 1htr in 1ch sp, [2ch, skip 1 st, 1htr in next st] twice, 3ch, ss in last 1ch sp from round 3.

Round 5: turn work over, 3dc in each of next 10 ch sps, (1dc, 3ch, 1dc) in leaf point ch sp, 3dc in each of next 10 ch sps, ss in last ch sp.

Round 6: turn work over, 3ch, 1dc in second dc from round 5, (3ch, 1dc) in each central dc in 3dc group from round 5 to leaf point, 3ch, 1dc in first dc in leaf point, [(3ch, 1dc) in leaf point ch sp] twice, 3ch, 1dc in next dc in leaf point, (3ch, 1dc) in each central dc in 3 dc group from round 5 along other side of leaf, 3ch, ss in ch sp from beg of round 4.

Trim and sew in ends.

FRILLY EDGE LEAF

Materials

Larger Leaf

- 0.75mm-1mm (14/10-12/6 steel) crochet hook
- Gütermann top stitching thread, colours used in this order: Fox Orange 982, Orange 350, Fawn 722, Light Green 152, Green 235
- Embroidery needle

Finished size

25mm x 40mm (1in x 1½in)

Smaller Leaf

- 0.6mm (12 steel) crochet hook
- Gütermann hand quilting cotton in Mid Blue 5725
- Embroidery needle

Finished size

18mm x 29mm (¾in x 1⅛in)

Round 1: Make a magic ring, 3ch (counts as 1tr), tr2tog in ring, [(3ch, tr3tog) into ring] 5 times, 1ch, 1tr in top of beg 3ch to finish.

Round 2: Change colour, *3ch (counts as 1tr), 2tr in same st sp, (3ch, 3tr) in each of next 3 ch sps, 4ch, 3tr in same ch sp (makes leaf point), (3ch, 3tr) in each of next 3 ch sps, 2ch, 1tr into top of beg 3 ch to make second leaf point and finish.

Round 3: Change colour, 2dc in leaf point st sp, *1dc between each of the 3 tr from previous round**, 3dc in 3ch sp, rep from * to bottom leaf sp, ending last rep at ** (19 dc so far), (2dc, 2ch, 2dc) in leaf point ch sp, rep from * up other side of leaf to beg leaf point, ending last rep at ** (40 dc so far), 2dc in beg leaf point ch sp, 1ch, 1htr in beg dc to make leaf point and finish.

Round 4: Change colour, 1dc in leaf point sp, 1dc in each st to bottom leaf point (22 dc so far), (1dc, 2ch, 1dc) in bottom leaf point ch sp, 1dc in each st up other side of leaf (45 dc so far), 1dc in beg leaf point sp, 1ch, 1htr in beg dc to make leaf point and finish.

Round 5: Change colour, 1dc in leaf point sp, *(3ch, skip 1 st, 1dc in next st) along side of leaf to bottom leaf point (12 dc, 11 ch sps), 3ch, (1dc, 4ch, 1dc) in leaf point sp, (13 ch sps so far), rep from * to beg leaf point, (24 ch sps so far), 3ch, 1dc in leaf point ch sp, 2ch, 1tr in beg dc to make leaf point and finish.

Trim and sew in ends.

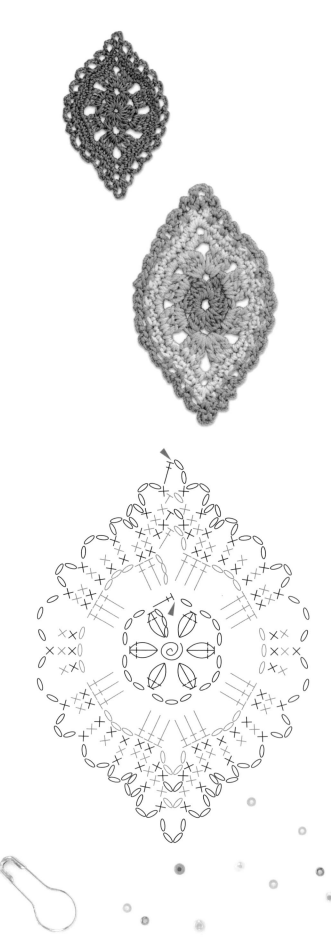

FIVE POINT LEAF

Materials

Larger Leaf

- 0.75mm-1mm (14/10-12/6 steel) crochet hook
- Gütermann top stitching thread in Light Green 152
- Embroidery needle

Finished size

23mm x 23mm (⅞in x ⅞in)

Smaller Leaf

- 0.6mm (12 steel) crochet hook
- Gütermann hand quilting cotton in Mid Blue 5725
- Embroidery needle

Finished size

15mm x 15mm (⅝in x ⅝in)

Round 1: Make a magic ring, 12dc into ring, ss in beg dc.

Round 2: Turn work over, 5ch, skip 1 dc, 2dtr in next dc, *[4ch, skip 1 dc, 2dtr in next dc] 3 times, 5ch, skip 1 dc, ss in next dc (4 spokes, 5 sps, 1 unworked dc from round 1).

Round 3: turn work over and work in the sps not the sts, *2ch, (5tr, 2ch, ss in last tr worked (makes picot), 2tr) in first sp, 1ch, ss between 2 dtr sts from round 2 (makes 1 leaf point), rep from * in next sp, 2ch, (4tr, 2ch picot, 3tr) in next sp, 2ch, ss between 2 dtr sts, **1ch, (3tr, 2ch picot, 4tr) in next sp, 2ch***, ss between 2 dtr sts, rep from ** to *** once, ss in first dc from round 1 (5 leaves, each with 7 tr and 1 picot).

Trim and sew in ends.

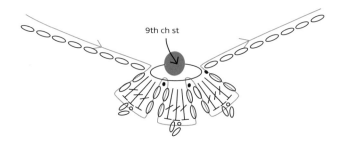

IVY STRAND

Materials

- 0.75mm (14/10 steel) crochet hook
- Gütermann top stitching thread in Eucalyptus Green 925
- Gütermann seed beads in Green 773875 (optional)
- Thin bead threading needle (optional)
- Embroidery needle

Finished size

20mm (¾in) per repeat, 10mm (⅜in) tall

One repeat of this pattern measures approximately 2cm (¾in) and uses one seed bead. The first step in making this strand is to thread more seed beads than needed (as you cannot thread extra beads on once you start crocheting). It's much better to have too many than not enough.

Step 1: Thread more seed beads than needed onto the thread.

Step 2: 9ch, trapping 1 seed bead in last ch.

Step 3: *(2ch, 2tr, 2ch, ss in last tr worked (makes picot), 1tr, 2ch, ss) in ch with bead, rep from * twice to make 3 point leaf.

Rep from step 2 until desired length of strand is achieved, 9ch to finish. Trim and sew in ends.

IVY LEAF

Materials

- 0.75mm-1mm (14/10-12/6 steel) crochet hook
- Gütermann top stitching thread in Green 235
- Embroidery needle

Finished size

22mm x 22mm (⅞in x ⅞in)

Round 1: Make a magic ring, 3ch, [(1tr, 1ch) into ring] 7 times, (1tr, 3ch, ss) into ring.

Round 2: Turn work over, 3ch, (3htr, 2ch, 1htr) in beg 3ch sp, skip 1 ch sp, (3tr, 2ch, 2tr) in next ch sp, miss 1 ch sp, (3dtr, 4ch, 3dtr) in next ch sp, miss 1 ch sp, (2tr, 2ch, 3tr) in next ch sp, miss 1 ch sp, (2htr, 2ch, 3htr) in last 3ch sp, 3ch, ss in magic ring.

Round 3: Turn work over, 2ch, 2dc in first ch sp, 1dc between each of next 3 tr, (2htr, 2ch, 1htr, 1dc) in next 2ch sp (makes leaf point), ss between htr and tr from round 2, 2ch, (3tr, 2 ch, 2tr) in next 2ch sp, ss between tr and dtr, 1ch, (2tr, 2dtr, 2ch, 2dtr, 2tr) in leaf point 4ch sp, 1ch, ss between dtr and tr, (2tr, 2ch, 3tr) in next 2ch sp, 2ch, ss between tr and htr, (1dc, 1htr, 2ch, 2htr) in next 2ch sp, 1dc between each of next 3 tr, 2dc in last 3ch sp, 2ch, ss in magic ring to finish.

Trim and sew in ends.

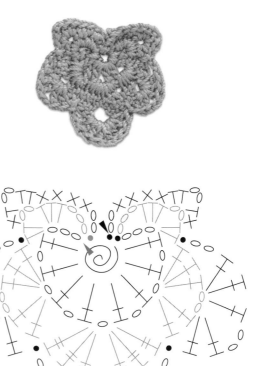

Ivy strand bracelet

This bracelet is not just a cute quick make. It can be scaled up by using different yarns and hook sizes to make other items such as necklaces, seasonal wreaths and decorative garlands for the home.

BEFORE STARTING....

The important first step in making this strand is to thread more seed beads than needed (as you cannot thread extra beads on once you start crocheting). It's much better to have too many than not enough so you can make it longer if needed.

Materials

- 0.75mm-1mm (14/10-12/6 steel) crochet hook
- Gütermann top stitching thread in Green 235
- Gütermann seed beads in Green 773875 (or any preferred beads of similar size)
- Thin bead threading needle
- Small jewellery pliers
- Jump rings (at least 3)
- Chain extender, or extra jump rings
- 2 Calotte crimps
- Jewellery clasp, such as a lobster claw or spring ring.
- Clear nail varnish or glue
- Embroidery needle

Finished size

195mm (7¾in) long including jewellery findings

This project incorporates beads but they are not essential. It is a great introduction to using a variety of jewellery findings.

One repeat of this pattern measures approximately 2cm (¾in) and uses one seed bead.

Follow the 3 steps listed for the Ivy Strand. Rep from step 2 a further 8 times, 9ch to finish. Trim and sew in ends.

To finish

Thread the last section of chain through a calotte, making sure the loops point away from the crochet leaves **(1)**.

Tie a knot in the end of the chain and secure with nail varnish or glue. Wait for the knot to dry and trim excess thread **(2)**.

Close the calotte with pliers, ensuring the knot is encased inside for a neat finish. The two loops should join to make one loop. Repeat on the other end of the bracelet **(3)**.

Use pliers to open and close a jump ring to secure the jewellery clasp to the calotte loop **(4)**.

Use pliers to open and close jump rings or a chain extender on the other end of the bracelet. Thread a few leftover beads onto the last jump ring for added decoration **(5)**.

Celestial

These are the crochet motifs you want to try out on a drizzly
Sunday under your favourite blanket and with a hot cup of
tea. Whether you prefer sunshine or rain, daytime or night
time, these motifs look fantastic on their own or paired
together as jewellery pieces. Many of the flat motifs can be
made into pillows by crocheting two and sewing them together
back to back, giving them a bit more weight for items like
dangly earrings or even a tiny baby-crib mobile! All use
Gütermann hand quilting cotton with a 0.5mm (12 steel) hook
or top stitching thread with a 0.75mm (14/10 steel) hook. A
0.9mm (14/8 steel) or 1mm (12/6 steel) hook can also be used
but will result in slightly bigger motifs.

LIGHTNING BOLT

Materials

- 0.75mm (14/10 steel) crochet hook
- Gütermann top stitching thread in Orange 350
- Embroidery needle

Finished size

28mm x 18mm (1⅛in x ¾in)

Row 1: Ch 10.

Row 2: 2dc in third ch from hook, 1dc in next 5 ch, dc2tog (8 sts).

Row 3: 1ch, turn, dc2tog, 1dc in next 5 sts, 2dc in last st.

Row 4: 1ch, turn, 2dc in first st, 1dc in next 5 sts, dc2tog.

Row 5: As row 3.

Row 6: 2ch (makes point), turn, 2dc in first st, 1dc in next 5 sts, dc2tog, ch3.

Row 7: 2ch (makes point) dc2tog over third and fourth ch from hook, 1dc in next 5 sts (6 sts).

Row 8: 1ch, turn, 2dc in first st, 1dc in next 3 sts, dc2tog.

Row 9: 1ch, turn, dc2tog, 1dc in next 3 sts, 2dc in last st.

Row 10: 2ch (makes point), 2dc in first st, 1dc in next 3 sts, dc2tog, 3ch.

Row 11: 2ch (makes point), dc2tog over third and fourth ch from hook, 1dc in next 5 sts.

Row 12: 1ch, turn, 2dc in first st, 1dc in next 3 sts, dc2tog.

Row 13: 1ch, turn, [dc2tog] twice, 1dc in next st, 2dc in last st (5 sts).

Row 14: 1ch, turn, 2dc in first st, 1dc in next 2 sts, dc2tog.

Row 15: 1ch, turn, 2dc2tog over next 4 sts, 2dc in last st. (4 sts)

Row 16: 1ch, turn, 2dc in first st, 1dc in next 2 sts, dc2tog.

Row 17: 1ch, turn, [dc2tog] twice, 1dc in last st (3 sts).

Row 18: 1ch, turn, dc2tog, dc2tog over st just worked and the last st (2 sts).

Row 19: 1ch, turn, dc2tog, ss in last st to finish.

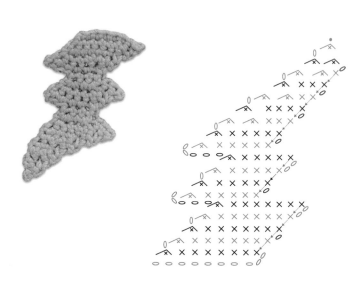

RAINDROP

Materials

- 0.5mm (12 steel) crochet hook
- Gütermann hand quilting cotton in Blue 5725
- Embroidery needle

Finished size

20mm x 12mm (¾in x ½in)

Round 1: Make a magic ring, 7ch (counts as 1ttr), 2ttr, 3dtr, 9tr, 3dtr, 3ttr, 2ch, 1tr in 7ch sp.

Round 2: 1ch, 2dc in tr sp, 2dc between every st around raindrop shape, 2dc in 2ch sp, 2ch, 1tr in beg 1ch sp.

Round 3: 1ch, 2dc in tr sp, 1dc in every st around raindrop shape, 2dc in 2ch sp, 2ch, 1tr in beg 1ch sp, ss to finish.

CLOUD

Materials

- 0.75mm (14/10 steel) crochet hook
- Gütermann top stitching thread in Cream 001
- Embroidery needle

Finished size

22mm x 12mm (⅞in x ½in)

Round 1: Make a magic ring, 3ch, 1htr, pull magic ring taut (makes loop), 3ch, htr in 3ch sp to make second loop, repeat to make 3 more loops.

Round 2: Down one side of loops work (2ch, 6tr) in first loop, ss in second loop, (3ch, 6dtr) in third loop, (3ch, ss) in fourth loop, (6tr, 2ch, ss) in fifth loop, working down other side of loops work (2ch, 6tr) in fifth loop, skip fourth loop, ss in third loop, skip second loop, (6tr, 2ch, ss) in first loop.

Round 3: (1ch, 1ss) between every st and (1ch, 1ss) in every 2ch sp around cloud. For crisp inner corners work (1ch, ss) into round 1 loops.

RAINBOW

Materials

- 0.5mm (12 steel) crochet hook
- Gütermann hand quilting cotton, colours used in this order: Purple 3832, Royal Blue 5725, Turquoise 6934, Green 8816, Yellow 758, Orange 2045, Red 2074
- Embroidery needle

Finished size

21mm x 21mm (¾in x ¾in)

Crochet in excess threads as you work, this strengthens the piece, makes the back neater, and means you only have to sew in 2 threads. Row 7 on the chart shows how this should be done, but work it on all rows.

Row 1: Make a magic ring leaving a long thread, 9dc in ring, ss to finish. Do not pull the ring too tight, there should be an arc shape left in the centre (9 sts).

Row 2: Change colour, (ss, 2dc) in first st, 2dc in every st, ss in first dc to finish (18 sts).

Row 3: Change colour, (ss, 1dc) in first st, 1dc every st, ss in first dc to finish.

Row 4: Change colour, (ss, 1dc) in first st, 2dc in next st, *1dc, 2dc in next st, rep from * to end, ss in first dc to finish (27 sts).

Row 5: Change colour, (ss, 1dc) in first st, 1dc in every st, ss in first dc to finish.

Row 6: Change colour, (ss, 1dc) in first st, 1dc, 2dc in next st, *2dc, 2dc in next st, rep from * to end, ss in first dc to finish (36 sts)

Row 7: Change colour, (ss, 1dc) in first st, 1dc in every st, ss in first dc to finish.

Trim all threads except the purple thread from row 1 (which would tighten the magic ring) and use that for sewing the centre arc together using a whip stitch.

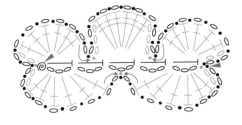

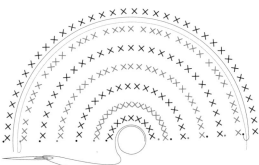

SUN

Materials

- 0.5mm (12 steel) crochet hook
- Gütermann hand quilting cotton, colours used in this order: Yellow 758, Mustard Yellow 956; **For embroidery:** Orange 2045
- Embroidery needle

Finished size

20mm x 20mm (¾in x ¾in)

Round 1: Make a magic ring, 10dc in ring, ss to first dc (10 sts).

Round 2: 2dc in every st (20 sts)

Round 3: *1dc, 2dc in next st, rep from * to end, ss in first dc (30 sts).

Round 4: *2dc, 2dc in next st, rep from * to end, ss in first dc (40 sts).

Round 5: 1dc in every st ss in first dc.

Round 6: 1dc in every st, ss in first dc.

Round 7: Change colour, ss in any dc, *skip 1 st, (2tr, 2ch, 2tr) in next st, skip 1 st, ss in next st, rep from * 11 times, ss in beg dc to finish.

Round 8: Change colour, ss surface crochet in every alternate st (shown as red dots on chart).

Using Orange embroider a smile and eyes in the stitches of round 4 as shown.

STAR

Materials

- 0.5mm (12 steel) crochet hook
- Gütermann hand quilting cotton, colours used in this order: Orange 2045, Mustard Yellow 956, Yellow 758, Light Ivory 919
- Embroidery needle

Finished size

20mm x 20mm (¾in x ¾in)

Round 1: Make a magic ring, 2ch (counts as htr), 2htr, 3ch, [3htr, 3ch] 3 times, ss in 2ch to finish.

Round 2: Change colour, ss in 3ch sp, 2ch (counts as htr), (2htr, 3ch, 3htr) in same 3ch sp, (3htr, 3ch, 3htr) in next 4 ch sps, ss in beg 2ch to finish.

Round 3: Change colour, ss between 2ch sp and last htr from round 2, *(3tr, 2ch, 3tr) in next 3ch sp, ss between next third and fourth htr from round 2, rep from * 4 times, ss in beg sp to finish.

Round 4: Change colour, 1dc in star tip ch sp *2dc in next 3 sps between sts, ss between next third and fourth htr from round 2, 2dc in next 3 sps between sts, (1dc, 2ch, 1dc) in 2ch sp, rep from * 4 times omitting last dc, ss in first dc to finish.

MOON

Materials

- 0.5mm (12 steel) crochet hook
- Gütermann hand quilting cotton, colours used in this order: Grey 6506, Light Ivory 919, Dark Grey 5114
- Embroidery needle

Finished size

20mm x 20mm (¾in x ¾in)

Round 1: Make a magic ring, 10dc in ring, ss to first dc (10 sts).

Round 2: 2dc in every st (20 sts)

Round 3: *1dc, 2dc in next st, rep from * to end, ss in first dc (30 sts).

Round 4: *2dc, 2dc in next st, rep from * to end, ss in first dc (40 sts).

Round 5: 1dc in every st ss in first dc.

Round 6: Change colour, ss in seventeenth st to the right from ss of round 5, 1dc in next 6 sts, 1htr in next 2 sts, 2htr in next st, 1htr in next 2 sts, 1tr in next 3 sts, 1tr in round 4 dc directly beneath this st, 2tr in last dc of round 3, 1tr in next st, 2tr in next st, 1tr in next 2 sts, 1htr in next st, 2htr in next st, 1htr in next 3 sts, 1dc in next 8 sts, ss in next st.

Round 7: Turn work, 1ch, 1dc in next 14 sts, 1htr in next 11 sts, 1htr in next 12 sts, 1dc over round 6 ss into round 5, 1dc in next round 5 dc, ss into next st to finish.

Round 8: Change colour, starting at top tip of moon, 1dc in every st around moon to last dc (39 sts), 1htr in 1ch sp, 2htr in next round 5 dc after ss, 1htr in next 8 sts in round 5, 2htr in next round 5 dc, ss in beg dc to finish.

Using Dark Grey embroider a small smile just below the nose and a closed eye to the left of the nose as shown.

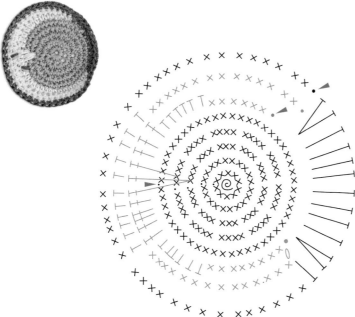

3D RAINBOW

Materials

- 0.5mm (12 steel) crochet hook
- Gütermann hand quilting cotton, colours used in this order: Dark Purple 3832, Mid Blue 5725, Turquoise 6934, Sage Green 8816, Yellow 758, Orange 2045, Bright Red 2074
- Embroidery needle
- Toy stuffing or thread scraps

Finished size

21mm x 10mm (¾in x ⅜in)

Round 1: Make a magic ring leaving a long thread, 18dc in ring, ss to finish. Do not pull the ring too tight, there should be an open circle left in the centre (18 sts).

Round 2: Change colour, (ss, 2dc) in first st, 2dc in every st, ss in first dc to finish (36 sts).

Round 3: Change colour, (ss, 1dc) in first st, 1dc every st, ss in first dc to finish.

Round 4: Change colour, (ss, 1dc) in first st, 2dc in next st, *1dc, 2dc in next st, rep from * to end, ss in first dc to finish (54 sts).

Round 5: Change colour, (ss, 1dc) in first st, 1dc in every st, ss in first dc to finish.

Round 6: Change colour, (ss, 1dc) in first st, 1dc, 2dc in next st, *2dc, 2dc in next st, rep from * to end, ss in first dc to finish (72 sts)

Round 7: Change colour, (ss, 1dc) in first st, 1dc in every st, ss in first dc to finish. Do not trim excess thread.

Fold circle in half so the end of round 7 lays on the corner of the rainbow shape. Use purple thread from round 1 to whip stitch the inner arc together. Crochet or sew the outer arc (round 7) together, either using (ss, 1ch) in each st, blanket stitch or whip stitch and stuffing as you go.

3D STAR PILLOW

Materials

- 0.5mm (12 steel) crochet hook
- Gütermann hand quilting cotton, colours used in this order: **Blue side**: Mid Blue 5725, Dusky Teal 7325, Mustard Yellow 956, Lime Green 9837, Dark Navy 5322; **Pink side**: Dusky Teal 7325, Dark Purple 3832, Lilac 4434, Mustard Yellow 956, Bright Pink 2955; **Border**: Mid Blue 5725
- Embroidery needle
- Toy stuffing or thread scraps

Finished size

20mm x 20mm (¾in x ¾in)

This motif is made in two halves which are then crocheted together. You can just make one half for a flat motif, or mix and match the colours so that both sides are either the same or completely different.

Half Star (make 2)

Round 1: Make a magic ring, 10dc in ring, ss to finish.

Round 2: Change colour, *1dc in next 2 sts, (1dc, 2ch, 1dc) in next st, rep from * 3 times, 1dc in next 2 sts, 2ch, ss in beg dc to finish.

Round 3: 1dc in a single dc from last round, *7tr (shell st) in next 2ch sp, 1dc in next single dc, rep from * 4 times omitting last dc and working ss in beg dc st to finish.

Round 4: Change colour, ss in fourth (centre) tr in any shell st, 2ch (counts as htr), 1htr in same st, *1dc in next 2 sts, 1dc in the next 2ch sps of round 2, 1dc in next 2 sts, (2htr, 2ch, 2htr) in centre tr of next shell st, rep from * 4 times omitting last 2 htr, ss in beg 2ch sp to finish.

Round 5: Change colour, (ss, 1dc) in 2ch sp, *1dc in next 4 sts, 1dc in single dc from round 2, 1dc in next 4 sts, (1dc, 2ch, 1dc) in 2ch sp, rep from *4 times omitting last dc, ss in beg dc.

Using Mid Blue crochet the 2 sides together using (ss, 1ch) in each st and (ss, 2ch, ss) in each 2ch sp star point, stuff with thread scraps or toy stuffing. Alternatively use blanket stitch or whip stitch to join together.

RINGED PLANET

Materials

- 0.75mm (14/10 steel) crochet hook
- Gütermann top stitching thread, colours used in this order: **Side 1**: Light Green 152, Lilac 158, Light Pink 758, Light Blue 714; **Side 2**: Lilac 158, Light Pink 758, Light Blue 714, Light Green 152; **Ring**: Bright Pink 382
- Embroidery needle
- Toy stuffing or 15mm bead

Finished size

18mm diameter (¾in)

This planet is a fun and quirky project that can be made into jewellery or sized up with thicker yarn for a cute plushie. It is constructed by crocheting two halves of the planet, sewing them together around a bead, and crocheting a ring around the seam. Using a large bead makes a consistent sphere shape and adds weight, but toy stuffing will work just as well if you do not have beads to hand.

Half Planet (make 2)

Round 1: Make a magic ring, 6dc in ring, ss in first dc (6 sts).

Round 2: 2dc in every st, ss in first dc to finish (12 sts).

Round 3: Change colour, *1dc, 2dc in next st, rep from * to end, ss in first dc (18 sts).

Round 4: *2dc, 2dc in next st, rep from * to end, ss in first dc to finish (24 sts).

Round 5: Change colour, *3dc, 2dc in next st, rep from * to end, ss in first dc (30 sts).

Round 6: 1dc in every st, ss in first dc to finish.

Round 7: Change colour, 1dc in every st, ss in first dc to finish.

Round 8: Change colour, 1dc in every st, ss in first dc to finish, leaving a long length of thread for sewing.

Whip stitch both halves together around a bead or toy stuffing. In the next round, when crocheting around the planet, insert hook in the same place as needle was inserted when sewing the two halves together.

Round 9: Using Bright Pink, work 1dc in each st around the seam, ss in first dc (30 sts).

Round 10: Work back-dc (crab st) in every st around ring, ss in first dc to finish.

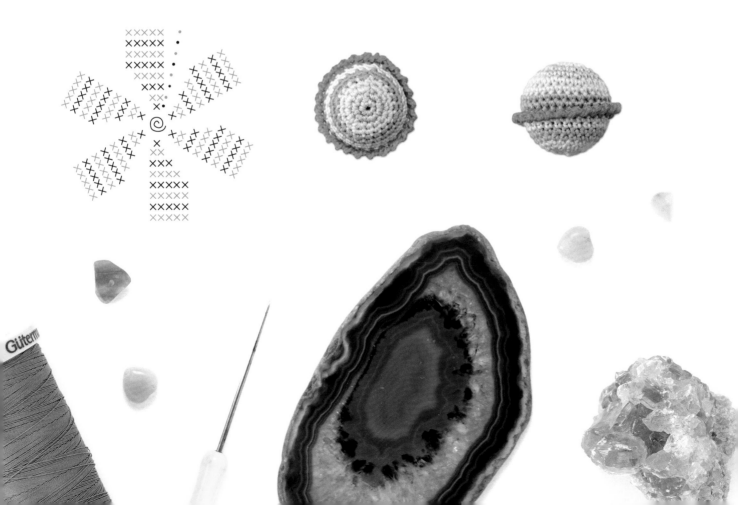

Mis-matched planet earrings

These earrings are perfect for when the world seems a little upside down and moving to another planet feels like a great idea. They are made in two halves and sewn together around a bead, to create perfect dangly spheres that are weighted. Mix and match different colours to create your own fantasy worlds.

Materials

- 0.75mm (14/10 steel) crochet hook
- Gütermann top stitching thread in colours of your choice
- 2 long flat head pins
- 2 ear wires
- Jewellery pliers
- 2 beads 15mm in diameter or toy stuffing
- Scissors
- Sewing needle

Finished size

18mm diameter (¾in)

Make 4 half planets in colours of your choice following the pattern for the Ringed Planet, and choose 2 of these to be the top of each planet **(1)**.

Thread flat head pin through a bead, then thread it through the magic ring of one of the chosen 'top' cups so it fits on the bead. Use pliers to make a loop and wrap the excess wire around it to make a bail. Trim excess wire **(2)**.

Fit the other half of the planet onto the bead and use whip stitch to sew the two halves together **(3)**.

When crocheting the ring around the planet, insert the hook in the same place as the needle was inserted when sewing the 2 halves together and work one round of dc as instructed in the pattern.

Work back-dc (crab st) as instructed in the pattern to finish **(4)**.

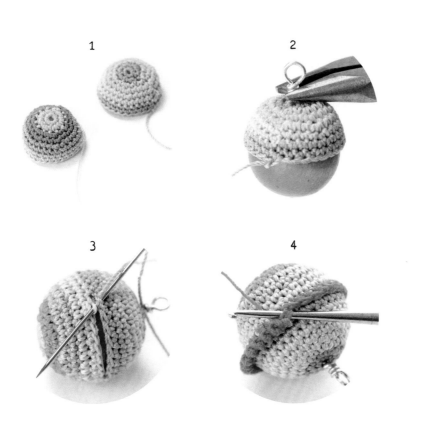

Food

Here is a good mix of 3D pieces and flat motifs, ideal for a tiny tea party, brunch, amigurumi, dollhouse décor or jewellery. Refer to the Techniques section for guidance on stuffing the cute 3D pieces.

The threads used are DMC fil à dentelles gauge 80 or Gütermann hand quilting cotton with a 0.5mm or 0.6mm (12 steel) hook. Also used is Gütermann top stitching thread with a 0.75mm (14/10 steel) or 0.9mm (14/8 steel) hook.

DOUGHNUT

Materials

- 0.5mm-0.6mm (12 steel) crochet hook
- DMC fil à dentelles gauge 80, colours used: Ecru, Purple 553; **For embroidery**: Fuchsia Pink 917, Mid Blue 798, Yellow 726
- Embroidery needle
- Chunky wool scraps for stuffing

Finished size

15mm x 15mm x 7mm (⅝in x ⅝in x ¼in)

Inner tube and top

Round 1: Using Ecru make a magic ring, 15dc in ring, ss to first dc, close the magic ring to make a loose 'O' shape.

Rounds 2 and 3: 1dc in each st, ss to first dc. This makes the inner tube of the doughnut. Skip these rounds if you want a flat motif.

Round 4: Change to Purple to start icing, working in a spiral from now on, 1dc in every st.

Round 5: *2dc, 2dc in next st, rep from * to end (20 sts).

Round 6: *3dc, 2dc in next st, rep from * to end (25 sts).

Round 7: *4dc, 2dc in next st, rep from * to end (30 sts).

Round 8: *5dc, 2dc in next st, rep from * to end, ss in next st to finish (35 sts).

Embroider little dashes on the icing using Fuchsia Pink, Mid Blue and Yellow.

Base

Round 1: Using Ecru, starting at the magic ring of round 1, work 1dc between each pair of sts, work in a spiral from now on (15 sts).

Round 2: 2dc in every st (30 sts).

Round 3: 1dc every st.

Round 4: *5dc, 2dc in next st, rep from * to end (35 sts).

Rounds 5 to 7: 1dc in every st.

At this point you will have a 'cotton reel' shape. Wind excess thread and chunky wool scraps around the doughnut 'inner tube' for easy stuffing. Use a whip stitch to sew the doughnut base to the back loops of the doughnut icing of round 8. Add extra stuffing as you go along.

(Optional) Finish the edge of the purple icing with surface ss along the back loops used to sew the two sides together. This can be done after stuffing if there are visible gaps between the stitches.

MACARON

Materials

- 0.5mm-0.6mm (12 steel) crochet hook
- DMC fil à dentelles gauge 80, colours used: **Body:** Purple 553 or Green 368; **Ganache:** Fuchsia Pink 917 or Ecru
- Embroidery needle
- Stuffing or yarn scraps

Finished size

7mm x 7mm x 5mm (¼in x ¼in x ¼in)

Body (make 2)

Round 1: Using colour for body make a magic ring, 2ch (does not count as htr), 10htr in ring, pull ring close, do not ss to finish (10 sts).

Round 2: 2dc in next 10 sts, invisible ss (see Techniques: Special Stitches) in first dc to finish (20 sts).

Ganache

Using Ecru for the Green and Fuchsia Pink for the Purple macaroon, work this round into the edge of one of the body pieces in the back loop only, 1dc in every st, invisible ss to finish (20 sts). Leave long length of thread.

Use excess thread to sew ganache stripe to other body piece, using a whip stitch to sew the back loops together and stuffing as you go.

(Optional) Ss surface crochet on the sewn back loops on both sides of the ganache stripes, invisible ss to finish.

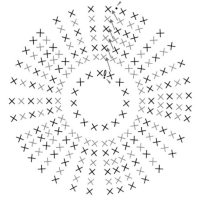

CARROT CAKE

Materials

- 0.5mm-0.6mm (12 steel) crochet hook
- DMC fil à dentelles gauge 80, colours used: Ecru, Tan Orange 976; **For embroidery**: Green 368
- Embroidery needle
- Stuffing or yarn scraps
- Disc of cardboard or plastic (optional)

Finished size

15mm x 15mm x 13mm (⅝in x ⅝in x ½in)

Cake Top

Round 1: Using Ecru make a magic ring, into ring work 2ch, 12htr, ss in beg 2ch.

Round 2: 3ch (change to Orange in third ch), *5tr popcorn st in next st, 1ch (change to Ecru), 3htr in next st, (change to Orange on last yarn over pull through in last st), rep from 5 times omitting last htr, ss in beg 2ch.

Round 3: Using Ecru, 2ch, *2htr in popcorn, 1htr in next 3 sts, rep from * 5 times omitting last htr, ss in beg 2ch to finish (30 sts).

Cake Base

Round 1: Using Ecru rep round 1 of cake top.

Round 2: 2ch, [2htr in next st, 3htr in next st] 6 times, ss in beg 2ch.

Round 3: 2ch, 1htr in every st, do not cut thread (30 sts).

If required, reinforce the base with a disc of cardboard or plastic.

Cake Sides

Continuing from the cake base, make 5ch, working in back loop only: ss in 2 sts of cake top, turn, 1dc in 5 ch sts back to base, working in back loop only: ss in 2 sts of cake base.

Continue working backwards and forwards to make 30 rows of 5 vertical sts around the cake. Stuff with scrap wool before closing.

To make a neat seam out of the first and last row of the cake sides, stitch the front or outer loops of last row to the ch sts of the first row.

Cream filing

Surface ss around the cake sides on the third st of each row.

Cake top icing edging

Using Ecru (ss, 2ch) in the back loops of the cake edge to disguise any gaps or stitch inconsistencies.

Carrot tops

Using Green, embroider the carrot top making a 'V' shape into each popcorn stitch.

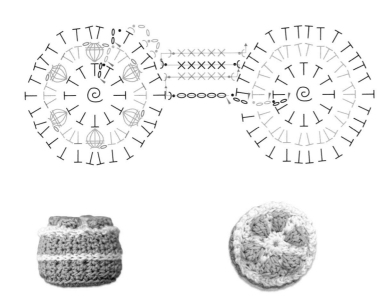

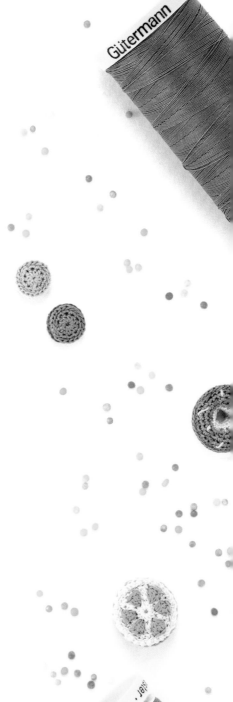

WATERMELON

Materials

- 0.5mm-0.6mm (12 steel) crochet hook
- Gütermann hand quilting cotton, colours used in this order: Red 2453, White 5709, Sage Green 8816, Dark Green 8113; **For embroidery**: Black 5201
- Embroidery needle
- Stuffing or yarn scraps

Finished size

15mm x 8mm (⅝in x ¼in)

This pattern is crocheted in a spiral and is stuffed with scrap yarn. An option for this pattern is to skip the last sewing up step and make a flat circular watermelon slice instead.

Round 1: Make a magic ring, 10dc in ring, pull magic ring closed, do not ss to join (10 sts).

Round 2: 2dc in every st (20 sts).

Round 3: 1dc in every st.

Round 4: (1dc, 2dc in next st) to end (30 sts).

Round 5: (2dc, 2dc in next st) to end (40 sts).

Round 6: (3dc, 2dc in next st) to end, ss in next st to finish (50 sts).

Round 7: Change colour, begin in last st of prev round, (4dc, 2dc in next st) to end, ss in next st to finish (60 sts).

Round 8: Change colour to sage green, 1dc in every st.

Embroider little black dashes for the pips. These can be worked evenly or randomly depending on your preference. For even placement of the stitches, begin each dash on row 3 spaced 1 stitch apart, and place the tops of the stitches on row 4, 2 stitches apart.

Stuffing

Using Dark Green thread fold the watermelon in half and ss into right hand corner st, (ss, 1ch) along the edge, trapping both sides of the 'V' of each st as you go. Stuff with yarn scraps half way through, and again as the hole begins to close. Finish with a ss and sew in ends.

VENETIAN SLICE

Materials

- 0.5mm-0.6mm (12 steel) crochet hook
- DMC fil à dentelles gauge 80, colours used: **Body**: Tan Orange 976, White B5200; **For embroidery**: Brown 433
- Embroidery needle

Finished size

10mm x 8mm x 6mm (⅜in x ¼in x ¼in)

Pastry

Row 1: Using Orange 6ch, 1dc in second ch from hook, 1dc in next 4 sts (5 sts).

Row 2: 1ch, turn, 5dc.

Rows 3 to 26: 1ch, turn, 5dc, ss to finish after row 26, leaving a long length of excess thread. Fold piece into 3 sections to make a thick stack and sew them together with excess thread.

Icing

Row 1: Using White, 1dc in second ch from hook, 1dc in next 3 sts (4 sts).

Row 2: 1ch, turn, 4dc.

Rows 3 to 8: 1ch, turn, 4dc, ss to finish after row 8, but do not cut yarn.

2dc in next st down side, 1dc in each of the next 5 row ends, going over the ch sts of first row work 3dc in corner st, 1dc in next 2 dc, 3dc in next corner st, 1dc in each of the next 5 row ends along next side, 2dc in next st, invisible ss in last st of row 8. Leave excess length for sewing.

Using Brown, embroider a zigzag pattern onto the white rectangle. Use excess white thread to sew the back loops of the white border to the top layer of the pastry.

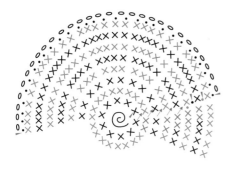

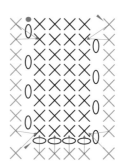

CUCUMBER SANDWICH

Materials

- 0.5mm-0.6mm (12 steel) crochet hook
- DMC fil à dentelles gauge 80, colours used: White B5200, Tan Orange 976, Green 368
- Embroidery needle
- Stuffing or yarn scraps

Finished size

10mm x 10mm x 4mm (⅜in x ⅜in x ¼in)

Bread (make 2)

Row 1: Using White make a magic ring, 1ch, 2dc (2 sts).

Row 2: 1ch, turn, 2dc in next 2 sts (4 sts).

Row 3: 1ch, turn, 2dc in first st, 1dc in every st to last st, 2dc in last st (6 sts).

Row 4: Rep row 3 (8 sts).

Row 5: Rep row 3, ss to finish (10 sts).

Crust

Using Orange (ss, 1ch) in every st down side of triangle, [ss, 1ch] 3 times in magic ring, (ss, 1ch) in every st up other side of triangle.

Cucumber filling

Using Green, rep rows 1 to 3 of bread. (6 sts)

Row 4: Turn work, *(4ch, 4dtr, 4ch, ss) in first st, ss in next 2 sts, rep from twice, ending with ss in the sixth st making 3 cucumber 'layers'.

Let the layers overlap each other and sew in place if needed.

Stack 2 bread layers on either side of the cucumber layer and sew together with white thread.

FRIED EGG

Materials

- 0.5mm-0.6mm (12 steel) crochet hook
- DMC fil à dentelles gauge 80, colours used in this order: Yellow 726, White B5200
- Embroidery needle

Finished size

13mm x 13mm (½in x ½in)

Round 1: Make a magic ring, 15dc in ring, ss in first dc to finish (15 sts).

Round 2: Change colour, 1dc in every st, ss in first dc.

Round 3: 5tr in first st, 1dc, 2tr in next st, 2dtr in next st, 2tr in next st, 1dc, 5tr in next st, 1dc, 1ch, 3dtr in next 2 sts, 2htr in next st, 2tr in next st, 2dtr in next st, 2tr in next st, ss in first tr to finish.

AVOCADO

Materials

- 0.5mm-0.6mm (12 steel) crochet hook
- Gütermann hand quilting cotton, colours used in this order: Brown 1833, Mid Green 8724, Lime Green 9837
- Embroidery needle

Finished size

12mm x 10mm (½in x ⅜in)

Round 1: Make a magic ring, 2ch, 11htr, invisible ss (see General Techniques: Special Stitches) in first htr to finish.

Round 2: Change colour, (ss, 2ch, 1htr) in first st of, 2htr in next 3 sts, 2tr in next st, 3dtr in next 2 sts, 2tr in next st, 2htr in next 3 sts, 2htr in invisible ss, invisible ss in first htr to finish.

Round 3: Change colour, (ss, 1dc) in invisible ss, 1dc in every st, finish with invisible ss in first dc.

TEAPOT

Materials

- 0.75mm (14/10 steel) crochet hook
- Gütermann top stitching thread, colours used: **Disc of tea**: Light Brown 139; **Teapot**: Light Blue 143; **For embroidery**: Bright Pink 382, Light Pink 758, Light Green 152
- Bead embroidery needle
- Stuffing or yarn scraps
- Small silver bead

Finished size

12mm x 10mm x 8mm (½in x ⅜in x ¼in)

Disc of tea

Round 1: Make a magic ring, 2ch, 15htr in ring, invisible ss in first htr to finish (15 sts).

Base

Round 1: Make a magic ring, 1ch, 10dc in ring, pull the magic ring closed but do not ss to finish round (10 sts).

Round 2: *1dc, 2dc in next st, rep from * to end, ss in first dc (15 sts).

Round 3: Working in back loops only, *2dc, 2dc in next st, rep from * to end, ss in first dc (20 sts).

Round 4: *3dc, 2dc in next st, rep from * to end, ss in first dc (25 sts).

Rounds 5 to 7: 1dc in every st, ss in first dc to finish each round.

Round 8: *3dc, dc2tog, rep from * to end (20 sts).

Round 9: *2dc, dc2tog, rep from * to end (15 sts). Stuff the teapot and sew the disc of tea onto the inner loops of this round.

Round 10: Working in front loops only, 1dc in every st.

Round 11: (Ss, 1ch) in every st.

(Optional) Working in front loops only (ss, 1ch) in each st around the base.

Embroider flowers and leaves on the front of the teapot.

Lid

Make a magic ring, 2ch (counts as htr), 10htr in ring, invisible ss in beg st. Sew a silver bead into the centre to make it easy to pick up.

Handle

Ss in beg of round 7 or 8, (2ch, htr) in same st (makes small loop), (2ch, 1htr) in ch sp (makes second loop), repeat to make 3 loops and ss to finish. Use thread end to sew the other end of handle further down the teapot.

Spout

Ss in round 4 on the other side of teapot from the handle, (2ch, 2htr) in same st, 2ch, turn, htr2tog, ss in same st. Sew in one excess thread, use other excess thread to sew base of spout in position so that the spout faces upwards.

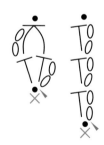

CUPPA TEA

Materials

- Embroidery needle
- Stuffing or yarn scraps

Small Cup

- 0.5mm-0.6mm (12 steel) crochet hook
- DMC fil à dentelles gauge 80, colours used: **Disc of tea**: Fawn Brown 435; **Cup**: Light Blue 800

Large Cup

- 0.75mm (14/10 steel) crochet hook
- Gütermann top stitching thread, colours used: **Disc of tea**: Light Brown 139; **Cup:** Light Blue 143

Finished size

5mm x 5mm x 8mm (¼in x ¼in x ¼in)

Disc of tea

Round 1: Make a magic ring, 2ch, 15htr in ring, invisible ss in first htr to finish (15 sts).

Base

Round 1: Make a magic ring, 1ch, 10dc in ring, pull the magic ring closed but do not ss to finish round (10 sts).

Round 2: *1dc, 2dc in next st, rep from * to end, ss in first dc (15 sts).

Round 3: Working in back loops only, *2dc, 2dc in next st, rep from * to end, ss in first dc (20 sts).

Rounds 4 to 6: 1dc in every st, ss in first dc to finish each round.

Round 7: *3dc, dc2tog, rep from * to end (16 sts). Stuff the cup and sew the disc of tea onto the inner loops of this round.

Round 8: Working in back loops only, 1dc in every st, ss to finish.

Handle

(2ch, htr) in last st of round 6, (makes small loop), (2ch, 1htr) in ch sp (makes second loop), repeat to make 3 loops and ss to finish. Use thread end to sew the other end of handle further down the cup.

Amigurumi cake slice

Gluten-free, dairy-free, nut-free and vegan.
They might be more a feast for the eyes than
the tummy, but once you make one cake you might
want to make all six and see how wonderfully
they fit together. Individualize each one with
embroidered faces, decoration or even initials
if this is a keepsake gift.

Materials

- 0.75mm (14/10 steel) crochet hook
- Gütermann top stitching thread, colours used: White 800, Light Pink 758, Bright Pink 382; **For embroidery**: Light Blue 143, Blue 322, Yellow 106, Bright Pink 382, Light Pink 758
- Scissors
- Sewing needle
- Toy stuffing or yarn scraps
- Small strip of card or plastic to reinforce stuffing, approximately 3cm x 8mm (1⅛in x ¼in), trimmed to fit (optional)

Finished size

20mm x 15mm x 15mm (¾in x ⅝in x ⅝in)

Top and back of cake

Row 1: Using White make a magic ring, into ring work 1ch, 1dc, pull to a loose close.

Row 2: 1ch, turn, 2dc in next st.

Rows 3 to 9: 1ch, turn, 1dc in every st to last st, 2dc in last st (9 sts).

Row 10: Working around the triangle, 1ch, 8dc evenly down side of triangle, (1dc, 1ch, 1dc) in magic ring, 8dc evenly up other side of triangle, 1ch, ss in beg ch of row 9.

Row 11: 1ch, working in back loop only, 1dc in next 9 sts at top of triangle.

Rows 12 to 16: 1ch, turn, 1dc in next 9 sts.

Repeat rows 1 to 10 of the top of the cake to make another triangle for the cake base **(1)**.

Sides of cake

Using Light Pink ss in ch at top right corner of base, 5ch, ss in top left corner of cake top, ss in next st in back loop only, turn, 1dc in each of the 5 ch sts back to base, ss in 2 sts of cake base in back loop only, continue working backwards and forwards to make rows of 5 vertical sts on two sides of the cake for the sponge cake sides **(2)**.

Before stuffing and sewing embroider the funfetti or an animal face. Reinforce the sides of the cake by cutting and folding a long strip of card and placing it in the cake. Use excess thread to stitch down the sides at the back of the cake before stuffing with wool scraps, making sure the card strip is kept in place **(3)**.

Using Bright Pink surface ss around the cake sides on the third st of each row to make the jam and cream filling **(4)**.

Using Bright Pink (ss, 1ch) in the front loops of row 9 to make cake top icing edge. If making a face ears could be added here by working (ss, 2ch, 2tr, 2dc, 2ch, ss) in the first and last stitches of the row **(5)**.

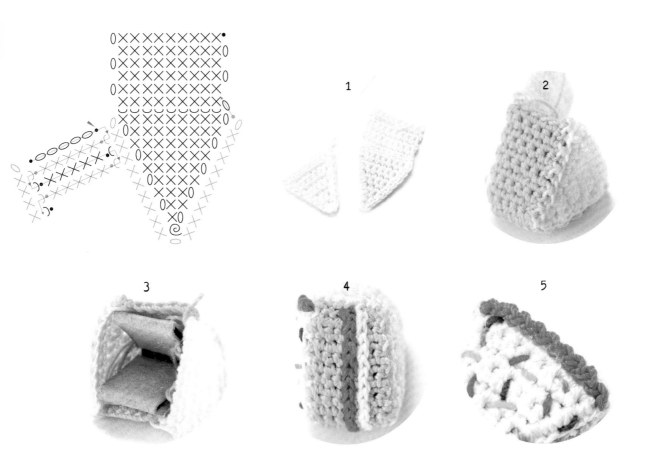

Blanket squares

The granny or blanket square ia a nostalgic crochet classic. Make tiny doll house blankets and clothing or one-off motifs for earrings and jewellery. They can be blocked, starched and framed for tiny artwork or even greetings cards. Check out the project at the end of this chapter to see how you can turn these motifs into tiny envelope pendants.

SCALLOPED SQUARE

Materials

- 0.75mm-1mm (14/10-12/6 steel) crochet hook
- Gütermann top stitching thread, colours used in this order: Dusky Pink 473, Bright Pink 382, Green 235, Red 156, Dusky Pink 473 (again)
- Embroidery needle

Finished size

23mm x 23mm (⅞in x ⅞in)

Round 1: Make a magic ring, (3ch (counts as 1tr), 1tr, 2ch) into ring, ([2tr, 2ch] 3 times) into ring, ss in beg 3ch to finish (makes square).

Round 2: Change colour, *ss in 2ch sp, (3ch, 2tr, 2ch, 2tr, 3ch, ss) in same 2ch sp, 3ch, rep from * in next 3 ch sps, ss in first 2ch sp to finish.

Round 3: Change colour, *ss in 3ch sp, (4ch, 3dtr, 2ch, 3dtr, 4ch, ss) in same 3ch sp, 4ch, rep from * in next 3 ch sps, ss in first 3ch sp to finish.

Round 4: Change colour, ss in 4ch sp, (4ch (counts as 1dtr), 1dtr, [2ch, 2dtr] 3 times) in same 4ch sp, *([2dtr, 2ch] 3 times, 2dtr) in next 4ch sp, rep from * twice, ss in beg 4ch to finish.

Round 5: Change colour, ss in ss sp from round 4, *4tr in next 2ch sp, 5tr in next 2ch sp, 4tr in next 2ch sp, 1dc between second and third tr, rep from * 3 times, omitting last dc, ss in ss sp from round 4.

Trim and sew in ends.

CLASSIC SQUARE WITH BORDER

Materials

- 0.6mm (12 steel) crochet hook
- Gütermann hand quilting cotton, colours used in this order: Lilac 4434, Light Lilac 4226, Dark Purple 3832
- Embroidery needle

Finished size

12mm x 12mm (½in x ½in)

This pattern has a reinforced border because it is designed with earrings in mind. Skip rounds 4 and 5 if you are making this for another purpose.

Round 1: Make a magic ring, (2ch (counts as 1htr), 2htr, 2ch) into ring, [(3htr, 2ch) into ring] 3 times, ss in beg 2ch to finish.

Round 2: Change colour, 2ch in corner sp (counts as 1htr), 2htr in same corner sp, 1ch, (3htr, 2ch, 3htr, 1ch) in each of next 3 corner sps, 3htr, 2ch, ss in beg 2ch in first corner sp to finish.

Round 3: Change colour, 2dc in corner sp, *1dc between next 3 sts, 2dc in ch sp, 1dc between next 3 sts, 3dc in corner sp, rep from * twice, 1dc between next 3 sts, 2dc in ch sp, 1dc between next 3 sts, 1dc in corner sp, ss in first dc.

Round 4: Turn work over, 1ch, rep round 3 (work sts into the same sps in round 2 as before, not into the sts of round 3), ss in beg 1ch sp.

Round 5: Turn work over, 1ch, 2dc in corner sp, rep round 3 (work sts into the same sps in round 2 as before), (2dc, 2ch, 2dc) in the corner sps for a sharper corner, 2dc in beg corner sp, 2ch, ss in first dc.

Trim and sew in ends. Attach jewellery findings to a 2ch sp on corner of granny square if making into earrings.

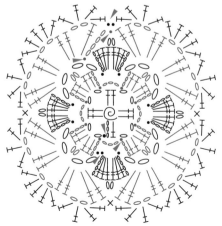

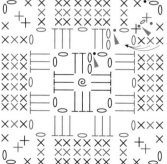

3D RUFFLE SQUARE

Materials

- 0.6mm (12 steel) crochet hook
- Gütermann hand quilting cotton, colours used in this order: Dusky Pink 2635, Dusky Teal 7325, Dark Red 2833, Sage Green 8816, Dusky Pink 2635 (again)
- Embroidery needle

Finished size

22mm x 22mm (⅞in x ⅞in)

Round 1: Make a magic ring, 12dc into ring, ss in beg dc.

Round 2: 8ch (counts as 1tr, 5ch), [(1tr, 5ch) into ring] 3 times, ss in third ch of 8ch sp to finish (4 segments).

Row 3 petals (red on chart): Change colour, ss in same third ch, 5ch, ss in next tr, do not repeat around piece.

Round 4 petals: 3ch, turn work, 8dtr in 5ch sp of round 2 and 3 together, 6dtr in 3ch sp (acts as 1tr on round 2), 1ch, ss in tr from beg of this short round.

Round 5 petals: 2ch, turn work, 2dc in 3ch sp, 2dc between each pair of dtr, 2dc in 1ch sp (30 dc so far), ss in same tr from beg of this short round (petal complete).

Repeat rounds 3 to 5 around remaining 3 segments to make 4 petals in total, starting with 5ch, ss in next tr.

Round 6: Working from the tr to the back of the petal clockwise, count the dc st, *ss in the fourteenth dc, 1dc in the same st, 1dc in next 2 sts, 1htr in next st, (2tr, 2ch, 2tr) in next st, 1htr in next st, 1dc in next 3 sts, 5ch, skip remaining dc from this petal; rep from *for the remaining 3 petals, ss in the beg dc to finish (turns petals into a square).

Round 7: (ss, 1dc) in 2ch corner sp, *1dc in next 6 sts, 5dc in 5ch sp, 1dc in next 6 sts, (1dc, 2ch, 1dc) in 2ch corner sp; rep from * 3 times omitting last dc in last rep, ss in beg dc.

Trim and sew in ends.

PUFF FLOWER SQUARE

Materials

- 0.6mm (12 steel) crochet hook
- Gütermann hand quilting cotton, colours used in this order: Dark Red 2833, Red 2453, Light Ivory 919, Dusky Blue 5815
- Embroidery needle

Finished size

20mm x 20mm (¾in x ¾in)

Round 1: Make a magic ring, 3ch (counts as 1tr), 1tr into ring, 1ch, [(2tr, 1ch) into ring] 7 times, ss in beg 3ch to finish.

Round 2: Change colour, ss in 1ch sp, 3ch (counts as 1tr), tr3tog in same ch sp, 2ch, (tr4tog, 2ch) in each of next 7 ch sps, ss in beg tr4tog to finish.

Round 3: Change colour, ss in 2ch sp, 4ch (counts as 1dtr), 3dtr in same ch sp, *4tr in next ch sp, (4dtr, 2ch, 4dtr) in next ch sp (corner); rep from * 3 times, omitting last 4 dtr on last rep, ss in beg 4ch to finish.

Round 4: Change colour, ss in 2ch corner sp, 1dc in same ch sp, *1dc in next 4 sts, 1dc between dtr and tr, 1dc in next 4 sts, 1dc between tr and dtr, (1dc, 2ch, 1dc) in 2ch corner sp; rep from * 3 times, omitting last dc on last rep, ss in beg dc.

Trim and sew in ends.

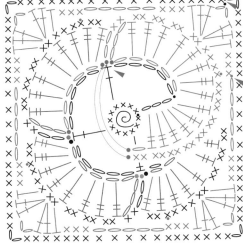

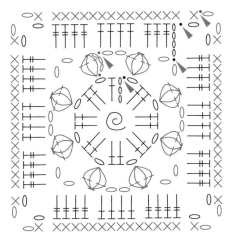

HEXAGON WHEEL

Materials

- 0.6mm (12 steel) crochet hook
- Gütermann hand quilting cotton, colours used in this order: Sage Green 8816, Turquoise 6934, Lilac 4434, Dark Purple 3832; **Surface crochet**: Dark Red 2833
- Embroidery needle

Finished size

30mm x 30mm (1⅛in x 1⅛in)

This piece involves some optional surface crochet (round 7 – highlighted in red on diagram) and should be the last round you crochet. The hexagon has a reinforced border because it is designed with earrings in mind, but you can skip rounds 4 and 6 if you are making this for another purpose.

Round 1: Make a magic ring, 4ch (counts as 1dtr), 1ch, ([1dtr, 1ch] 11 times) into ring, ss in beg 4ch to finish.

Round 2: Change colour, ss in any 1ch sp, 3ch (counts as 1tr), 1tr in same 1ch sp, *2tr in next 1ch sp, (2tr, 1ch, 2tr) in next 1ch sp (makes corner), rep from * 4 times, 2tr in next 1ch sp, 2tr in beg 1ch sp, 1ch, ss in beg 3ch to finish.

Round 3: Change colour, ss in any 1ch sp, 2dc in same 1ch sp, *2dc between each of the 6 tr along one side, 3dc in 1ch corner sp; rep from * 4 times, 2dc between each of the 6 tr along last side, 1dc in 1ch corner sp, ss in beg dc.

Round 4: Rep round 3, working the sts into the sps of round 2, not into the sts of round 3.

Round 5: Turn work over, change colour, (ss, 1dc) in central dc in ch sp from round 3, *dc in next st, [skip 1 st, 1dc in next st] 5 times, 1dc in next 2 sts, rep from * 5 times, omitting the last dc, ss in beg dc.

Round 6: Turn work over, 1ch, dc into the st sps of round 4 (if worked, if not round 3), not into the sts of round 5 as follows: 1dc in last dc of round 4 (very tip of hexagon corner), *1dc in next 7 sts, (1dc, 2ch, 1dc) in next dc (makes corner); rep from * 4 times omitting the last dc, ss in beg dc to finish.

Round 7: (Optional, highlighted in red on chart) Surface crochet, change colour, ss in each st of round 4 (or 3).

Trim and sew in ends.

FRILLY EDGE SQUARE

Materials

- 0.6mm (12 steel) crochet hook
- Gütermann hand quilting cotton, colours used in this order: Mid Blue 5725, Light Blue 6217, Dark Navy 5322, Dark Red 2833, Mustard Yellow 956
- Embroidery needle

Finished size

20mm x 20mm (¾in x ¾in)

Round 1: Make a magic ring, 8dc into ring, ss in beg dc to join.

Round 2: Change colour, 2dc in each st, ss in beg dc to finish (16 sts).

Round 3: Change colour, ss in any st, 3ch (counts as 1tr), tr2tog in same st, (3ch, tr3tog) in each alternate st, 3ch, ss in beg 3ch to finish (8 clusters, 8 ch sps).

Round 4: Change colour, ss in ch sp, *4dc in same ch sp, 1ch, 4dc in next ch sp, 2ch, rep from * 3 times, ss in beg dc to finish.

Round 5: Change colour, ss in 2ch sp, 4ch (counts as 1dtr), 2dtr in same sp, *5ch, ss in 1ch sp, 5ch, (3dtr, 2ch, 3dtr) in 2ch sp, rep from * twice, 5ch, ss in 1ch sp, 5ch, 3dtr in beg 2ch sp, 1ch, 1dc in 4ch to finish.

Round 6: Do not change colour, 1dc in corner sp, *4ch, (ss, 2ch, 3htr, 2ch, ss) in next 5ch sp, (ss, 2ch, 3htr, 2ch, ss) in next 5ch sp, 4ch, (1dc, 3ch, 1dc) in corner ch sp, rep from * 3 times omitting last dc on last rep, ss in beg dc.

Trim and sew in ends.

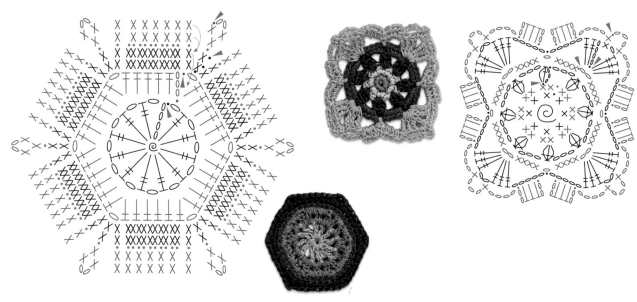

LACY GRANNY SQUARE

Materials

- 0.6mm (12 steel) crochet hook
- Gütermann hand quilting cotton, colours used in this order: Mustard Yellow 956, Dusky Pink 2635, Dark Red 2833, Dark Navy 5322, Mid Blue 5725
- Embroidery needle

Finished size

27mm x 27mm (1in x 1in)

Round 1: Make a magic ring, (2ch (counts as 1htr), 3htr, 2ch) into ring, ([4htr, 2ch] 3 times) into ring, ss in beg 2ch to finish.

Round 2: Change colour, ss in corner ch sp, (2ch, 3htr, 2ch, 4htr) in same 2ch sp, 2ch, (4htr, 2ch, 4htr, 2ch) in next 3 ch sps, ss in beg 2ch to finish.

Round 3: Change colour, ss in 2ch sp, (2ch, 3htr, 2ch, 4htr) in same ch sp, (4htr, 2ch, 4htr) in next 7 ch sps, ss in beg 2ch to finish.

Round 4: Change colour, ss in corner ch sp, (2ch, 3htr) in same ch sp, *5ch, ss in next 2ch sp, 5ch, (4htr, 2ch, 4htr) in corner sp, rep from * twice, 5ch, ss in next 2ch sp, 5ch, (4htr, 1ch) in beg corner ch sp, 1dc in beg 2ch so that crochet finishes at very tip of square.

Round 5: Do not change colour, *6ch, ss in next 5ch sp, 4ch, 1tr in next 2ch sp from round 3 below, 4ch, ss in next 5ch sp, 6ch, ss in corner 2ch sp; rep from * 3 times, working last ss in 1ch sp from round 4 to finish.

Round 6: Change colour, ss in 4ch sp to the left of any 1 tr in round 5, *2dc in 4ch sp, 3ch, 5dtr in next 6ch sp, 5ch, ss in first ch just made (makes corner picot), 5dtr in next 6ch sp, 3ch, 2dc in next 4ch sp; rep from * 3 times, ss in beg dc.

Trim and sew in ends.

FLORAL ENVELOPE SQUARE

Materials

- 0.6mm (12 steel) crochet hook
- Gütermann hand quilting cotton, colours used in this order: Dark Red 2833, Mid Blue 5725, Orange 2045, Dark Navy 5322, Mustard Yellow 956, Dark Red (again)
- Embroidery needle

Finished size

20mm x 20mm (¾in x ¾in)

Round 1: Make a magic ring, 2ch (counts as 1htr), 1htr into ring, 2ch, [(2htr, 2ch) into ring] 3 times, ss in beg 2ch to finish.

Round 2: Change colour, ss in any 2ch corner sp, 3ch (counts as 1tr), 7tr in same ch sp, 8tr in next 3 corner ch sps, ss in beg 3ch to finish (4 shells).

Round 3: Change colour, ss between 2 shell groups at beg of round 2, *1dc in next 8 sts, 1dc between 2 edge htr sts from shells in round 1 (separates shells into flower petals); rep from * 3 times, ss in beg dc to finish.

Round 4: Change colour, ss in last dc of round 3 (st that separates the petals), 3ch, 3dtr in same st, *skip 2 sts, 1dc in next 4 sts, (4dtr, 2ch, 4dtr) in next separating dc; rep from * 3 times, omitting last 4 dtr on last rep, 2ch, ss in beg 3ch to finish.

Round 5: Change colour, ss in 2ch corner sp from round 4, 1dc in same sp, *1dc in next 4 sts, 1dc in third dc of shell from round 3 (makes stripe), 1dc in next 2 sts, 1dc in sixth dc of shell from round 3, 1dc in next 4 sts, (1dc, 2ch, 1dc) in 2ch sp; rep from * 3 times, omitting last dc in last rep, ss in beg dc to finish.

Round 6: Change colour, ss in 2ch corner sp, 1dc in same sp, *1dc in next 4 sts, 1dc between dtr and dc in round 4 (makes stripe to right of round 5 stripe), 1dc in next 6 sts, 1dc between dc and dtr from round 4, 1dc in next 4 sts, (1dc, 2ch, 1dc) in 2ch corner sp; rep from * 3 times, omitting 1 ch in last corner and working last dc in beg dc so that thread is positioned at the very tip of the corner.

Trim and sew in ends.

CIRCLE SQUARE

Materials

- 0.6mm (12 steel) crochet hook
- Gütermann hand quilting cotton, colours used in this order: Light Blue 6217, Mid Blue 5725, Dark Navy 5322, Dusky Teal 7325
- Embroidery needle

Finished size

15mm x 15mm (⅝in x ⅝in)

Round 1: Make a magic ring, 4ch (counts as 1tr, 1ch), [(1tr, 1ch) into ring] 11 times, ss in beg 4ch to finish.

Round 2: Change colour, ss in any ch sp, 3ch (counts as 1tr), 1htr in same ch sp, *2dc in each of next 2 ch sps, (1htr, 1tr, 2ch, 1tr, 1htr) in next ch sp; rep from * 3 times, omitting last (1tr, 1htr) on last rep, ss in beg 3ch to finish.

Round 3: Change colour, (ss, 1ch, 1dc) in 2ch corner sp, *1dc in each st to 2ch corner sp, (1dc, 2ch, 1dc) in 2ch corner sp; rep from * 3 times, omitting last dc on last rep to finish.

Round 4: Change colour, rep round 3.

Trim and sew in ends.

HEXAGON ROSE

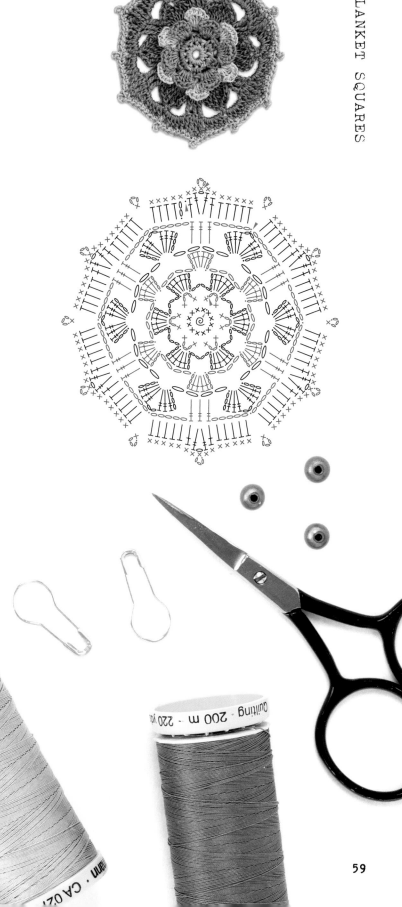

Materials

- 0.6mm (12 steel) crochet hook
- Gütermann hand quilting cotton, colours used in this order: Sage Green 8816, Lilac 4434, Dusky Pink 2635, Light Blue 6217, Emerald Green 8244, Mid Blue 5725, Lilac (again), Sage Green (again)
- Embroidery needle

Finished size

30mm x 30mm (1⅛in x 1⅛in)

Round 1: Make a magic ring, 12dc into ring, ss in beg dc to finish.

Round 2: Change colour, [1dc in next 2 sts, 3ch] 6 times, ss in beg dc to finish.

Round 3 petals: Change colour, *(ss, 3ch, 4tr, 3ch, ss) in 3ch sp of round 2, 4ch; rep from * 5 times, ss in beg 3ch sp to finish.

Round 4 petals: Change colour, rep round 3 into 4ch sps from round 3, ensuring the new 4ch sps between petals lay behind the petals of round 3, ss in beg 4ch sp to finish.

Round 5 leaves: Change colour, (ss, 3ch, 3dtr, 2ch, 3dtr, 3ch, ss, 4ch) in each of the six 4ch sps, ss in beg 4ch sp to finish.

Round 6: Change colour, *ss in leaf tip 2ch sp, 5ch, 3dtr in 4ch sp, 5ch; rep from * 5 times, ss in beg 5ch sp to finish.

Round 7: Change colour, ss in 5ch sp to the left of 3dtr in round 6, 2ch (counts as htr), 4htr in same 5ch sp, *5htr in next 5ch sp, 1tr in next dtr, (1dtr, 2ch, 1dtr) in next dtr, 1tr in next dtr, 5htr in next 5ch-sp; rep from * 4 times, 5htr in next 5ch sp, 1tr in next dtr, (1dtr, 2ch, 1dtr) in next dtr, 1tr in next dtr, ss in beg 2ch to finish.

Round 8 picot border: Change colour, 1dc in 1ch corner sp, *1dc in next 7 sts, 1dc between fifth and sixth htr of first petal from round 7, 3ch, ss in same dc (makes picot), 1dc in next 7 sts, (1dc, 3ch, ss in same dc) in 1ch corner sp, rep from * 5 times (working alternate picots between fifth and sixth htr of each petal), ss in beg dc of round.

Trim and sew in ends.

Envelope belt

purse and necklace

This project is perfect for keeping
special things close to you. Whether
you're storing money or keepsake notes,
this envelope can be scaled up and down
depending on the thread and hook used.

Materials

Belt Purse

- 2mm-2.5mm (4-2 steel) crochet hook
- Ricorumi DK cotton, colours used in this order: Fox 025, Aqua 074, Mustard 064, Fox (again), Pea 077, Burgundy 030, Aqua (again)
- Tapestry needle
- Button 15mm diameter

Finished size

90mm x 90mm (3½in x 3½in)

Adapt your purse with straps and handles or extra charms so that it's just as special as the special object inside it.

Necklace

- 0.6mm (12 steel) crochet hook
- Gütermann hand quilting cotton, colours used in this order: Orange 2045, Dusky Teal 7325, Mustard Yellow 956, Orange (again), Lime Green 9837, Dark Red 2833, Dusky Teal (again)
- Embroidery needle
- 2 jump rings
- Jewellery pliers
- 1 small bead, approx 3mm diameter
- Embroidery needle

Finished size

20mm x 23mm (¾in x ⅞in)

Front Panel

Follow instructions for the Floral Envelope Square.

Back Panel

Repeat rounds 1 to 6 as for front panel. You will now be working in rows.

Row 7 (RS): 1ch, 1dc in next 19 sts, 1dc in 2ch corner sp (20 sts).

Rows 8 to 10: Turn work, 1ch, 1dc in each st.

If you want the bag flap to be extra long add 2 to 4 more rows here.

Row 11: Turn work, 1ch, dc2tog, 1dc in next 16 sts, dc2tog (18 sts).

Rows 12 to 15: Turn work, 1ch, dc2tog, 1dc in each st to last 2 sts, dc2tog (10 sts).

Row 16: (Buttonhole) Turn work, 1ch, dc2tog, 1dc in next 2 sts, 3ch, skip 2 sts, 1dc in next 2 sts, dc2tog (9 sts).

Check at this point that your chosen bead or button will go through the hole, if the buttonhole is too small then increase the number of ch sts in the buttonhole.

Row 17: 1ch, dc2tog, 1dc in next st, 3dc in buttonhole ch sp, 1dc in next st, dc2tog (7 sts).

Row 18: Turn work, 1ch, dc2tog, 1dc in next 3 sts, dc2tog (5 sts), fasten off, weave in end and trim **(1)**.

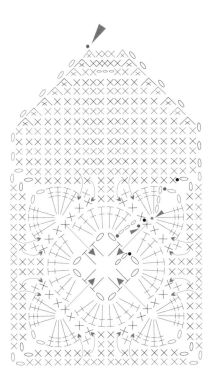

Joining Panels

This step involves using slip stitches to join the two sides together. Alternative methods can be used such as blanket stitch or whip stitch.

Lay the back panel wrong side up. Lay the front panel on top of the back panel, right side up, and line up the corner ch sps.

Working through both front and back panels together, ss in top left corner ch sp, *(1ch, 1ss) in each pair of sts down one side of the bag to join together **(2)**, (1ch, ss, 1ch, ss) in corner ch sp, rep from * for next 2 sides and 1 corner **(3)**. In the last top right corner, work (1ch, ss) through both panels, 1ch, ss through front panel only.

Working through front panel sts only, work (ss, 1ch) in each st across top of panel, ss in top left corner ch sp again.

Turn work to continue with the flap, (1ch, ss) in each row end up first side of flap, (1ch, ss) in each st along top, (1ch, ss) in each row end down second side of flap, 1ch, ss in top right corner of bag to finish. Sew button to top panel checking the buttonhole placement before sewing.

Belt Strap (optional)

Row 1: 9ch, leave a long length of yarn for sewing later – to make the bag strap wider, add more ch sts.

Row 2: 1dc in second ch from hook, 1dc in each remaining ch (8 dc).

Rows 3 to 17: turn work, 1ch, 1dc in each st.

Fasten off at end of row 17. Use yarn at top and bottom of strap to sew onto back of bag **(4)**.

Shoulder Strap (optional)

Ss through both panels in top right corner ch sp, (3ch, 1tr) in same sp (makes small loop), 3ch, 1tr into loop sp, cont until desired length is reached, ss in top left corner ch sp. Trim and sew in ends to finish.

Adding Findings for Necklace

Use a crochet hook to prise 2 holes in the centre of row 7 of the back panel so a jump ring can be threaded through. Attach another jump ring before closing with pliers **(5)**.

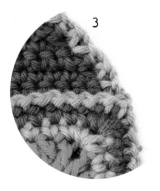

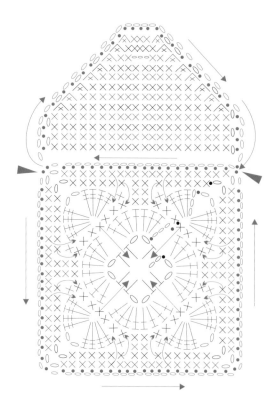

Sealife

Tiny motifs for your inner mermaid. The motifs use
Gütermann hand quilting cotton with a 0.5mm (12 steel)
hook or Gütermann top stitching thread with a 0.75mm
(14/10 steel) hook. A 0.9mm hook (14/8 steel) can also
be used but will result in slightly bigger motifs.

SPIRAL SHELL

Materials

- 0.5mm (12 steel) crochet hook
- Gütermann hand quilting cotton in Turquoise 6934
- Embroidery needle

Finished size

12mm x 12mm (½in x ½in)

Round 1: Make a magic ring, into ring work 5dc, 6htr, do not join.

Round 2: Continue in a spiral working in back loops only, 2htr in next 5 sts, 2tr in next 10 sts, 2dtr in next 2 sts, 1dtr in next 2 sts.

Round 3: 1back-dc (crab st) in every st to the last 3 sts of round 1, when you reach a stitch which has a dtr worked in it, continue with back-dc but work in front loop only to the fourth st from the beg of round 1, use needle to thread excess thread into second dc of round 1 for a neat finish to the spiral. Sew in and trim ends from the back of the shell.

STARFISH

Materials

- 0.5mm (12 steel) crochet hook
- Gütermann hand quilting cotton in Peach 2346
- Embroidery needle

Finished size

25mm x 25mm (1in x 1in)

Round 1: Make a magic ring, into ring work 6ch (counts as 1htr, 3ch), (2htr, 3ch) 4 times, 1htr, ss in third ch of beg 6ch sp to finish.

Round 2: 2ch (counts as 1htr), 5htr in 6ch sp, 6htr in next 4 3ch sps, ss in first htr.

Round 3: *9ch, starting in second ch from hook, 2dc, 3htr, 3tr (makes starfish arm) ss in fifth st in htr group, ss in next 3 sts, rep from * 4 times omitting last ss to create other 4 arms.

Round 4: *(1ch, ss) in 8 ch sts on side of arm, 3ch to make arm tip, (ss, 1ch) in 8 sts on other side of arm, (ss, 1ch) in the 4 sts from round 2 between each arm, rep from * 4 times omitting last ss and 1ch.

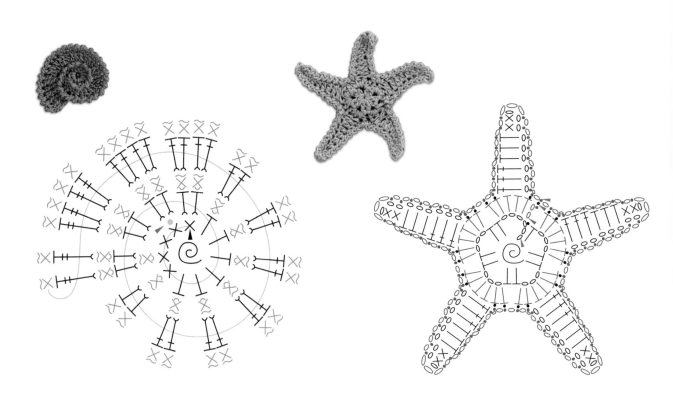

GOLDFISH

Materials

- 0.5mm (12 steel) crochet hook
- Gütermann hand quilting cotton, colours used: **Body**: Orange 2045; **Eyes**: Black 5201
- Embroidery needle

Finished size

20mm x 15mm x 8mm (¾in x ⅝in x ¼in)

Body

Round 1: Make a magic ring, into ring work 6dc, ss in first dc (6 sts).

Round 2: 1ch, [1dc, 2dc in next st] 3 times, ss in first dc (9 sts).

Round 3: 1ch, [2dc, 2dc in next st] 3 times, ss in first dc (12 sts).

Round 4: 1ch, 1dc in every st, ss in first dc.

Round 5: 1ch, [2dc, 2dc in next st] 4 times, ss in first dc (16 sts).

Round 6: 1ch, [2dc, 2dc in next st] 5 times, dc in last st, ss in first dc (21 sts).

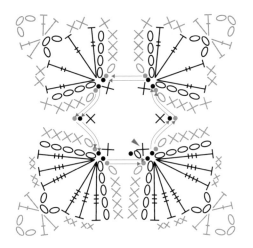

Round 7: 1ch, 1dc in next 2 sts, 1dc back loop only in the next 3 sts, 1dc in next 11 sts, 1dc back loop only in next 3 sts, 1dc in last 2 sts, ss in first dc.

Round 8: 1ch, 1dc in every st, ss in first dc.

Round 9: 1ch, [2dc, dc2tog] 5 times, dc in next st, ss in first dc (16 sts).

Begin lightly stuffing the fish shape.

Round 10: 1ch, [2dc, dc2tog] 4 times, ss in first dc (12 sts).

Round 11: 1ch, [2dc, dc2tog] 3 times, ss in first dc (9 sts).

Round 12: 1ch, [1dc, dc2tog] 3 times, ss in first dc (6 sts).

Tail fins

Round 13: Work (ss, 5ch, 2ttr, 1qtr, 3ch, 1qtr, 2ttr, 5ch, ss) in first st, ss in second st, (ss, 4ch, 2dtr, 3ch, 2dtr, 4ch, ss) in third and fourth st, ss in fifth st, (ss, 5ch, 2ttr, 1qtr, 3ch, 1qtr, 2ttr, 5ch, ss) in sixth st.

Round 14: (Ss, 1ch, 4dc) in 5ch sp, [2dc in sp between next 2 sts] twice, (1htr, 1tr, 3ch, 1tr, 1htr) in 3ch sp, [2dc in sp between next 2 sts] twice, 4dc in 4ch sp, 1ch, ss in first st from round 12, ss in next st from round 12, *ss in next st from round 12, 1ch, 4dc in 4ch sp, 2dc in next sp between next 2 sts, (1htr, 1tr, 3ch, 1tr, 1htr) in 3ch sp, 2dc in sp between next 2 sts, 4dc in 4ch sp, 1ch, ss in same st from round 12 as start of this fin, rep from * for next fin, ss in next st from round 12, ss in last st from round 12, (1ch, 4dc) in 5ch sp, [2dc in sp between next 2 sts] twice, (1htr, 1tr, 3ch, 1tr, 1htr) in 3ch sp, [2dc in sp between next 2 sts] twice, 4dc in 4ch sp, 1ch, ss in same st from round 12 as start of this fin.

Sew the 6 sts of round 12 together to finish.

Side Fins

Working in the 3 front loops on both sides of fish left from round 7, ss in first st, 2ch, (1tr, 2ch, 1tr) in second st, 2ch, ss in third st. Repeat for other side fin.

Top Fin

Working around the dc post of rounds 6, 7 and 8, ss in top of fish on round 6, 2ch, 1tr in same st, (1tr, 2ch, 1tr) in round 7 st, 1ch, ss in round 8 st.

Using Orange embroider a big puff on each side of the fish over rounds 3 and 4 – the more sts worked into the same place, the more goggly the eyes will look. Using Black embroider a small black eye on top of each puff.

SEAWEED

Materials

- 0.5mm (12 steel) or 0.75mm (14/10 steel) crochet hook
- Gütermann hand quilting cotton in Sage Green 8816 or Gütermann top stitching thread in Light Green 152 or Dark Green 472
- Embroidery needle

Finished size

5mm (¼in) wide, any length

Make a magic ring, into ring work (2ch, 1tr, 2ch, ss).

Row 1: *4ch, (1tr, 2ch, ss) in third ch from hook, rep from * until desired length is achieved. The last repeat makes the top of the seaweed.

Row 2: Working along other side of seaweed, ss in next ch, *(ss, 2ch, 1tr, 2ch, ss) in next ch, rep from * until magic ring is reached, (ss, 2ch, 1tr, 2ch, ss) in magic ring to finish.

TURTLE

Materials

- 0.5mm (12 steel) crochet hook
- Gütermann hand quilting cotton, colours used in this order: Sage Green 8816, Mid Green 8724, Fawn Brown 1225
- Embroidery needle

Finished size

20mm x 20mm (¾in x ¾in)

Round 1: Make a magic ring, into ring work 2ch (counts as 1 htr), 15htr, ss in first htr.

Round 2: 2ch (counts as 1 htr), 1htr in same st, 2htr in next 7 sts, (2htr, 2ch, 2htr) in next st, 2htr in next 7 sts, ss in beg 2ch.

Round 3: 2ch (does not count as htr), 1htr in same st, 1htr in next 17 sts, 3htr in 2ch sp, 1htr in every st to end, ss in beg 2ch.

Round 4: Change colour, working in front loops only, ss in second st of round 3, 1back-dc (crab st) in every st including the beg st where first ss is placed. Sew end through first back-dc for seamless border.

Round 5: Change colour, working in back loop of round 3 sts only, *(ss, 3ch, 1tr, 1dtr) in first htr of round 3, (1dtr, 1tr, 3ch, ss) in next st, ss in next 4 sts, (ss, 5ch, 2ttr, 5ch, ss) in next st, ss in next 8 sts, (ss, 3ch, 1tr, 3ch, ss) in next st, ss in next 7 sts, (ss, 3ch, 1tr, 3ch, ss) in next st, ss in next 8 sts, (ss, 5ch, 2ttr, 5ch, ss) in next st, ss in last 4 sts, ss in beg st to finish.

Using Mid Green, embroider hexagonal decoration onto shell.

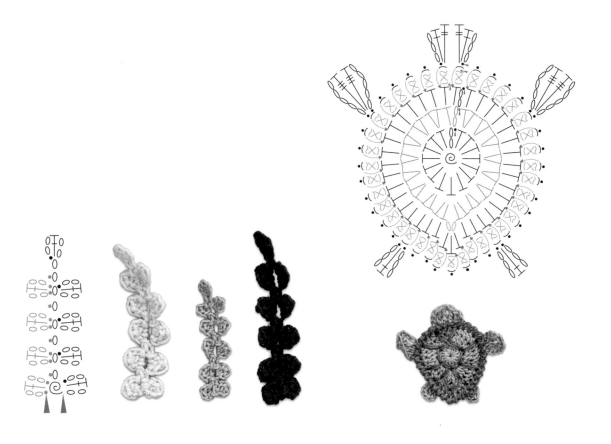

CLAM SHELL

Materials

- 0.75mm (14/10 steel) crochet hook
- Gütermann top stitching thread in Cream 414
- Embroidery needle

Finished size

16mm x 16mm (⅝in x ⅝in)

Round 1: Make a magic ring, into ring work 2ch, 6tr, 2ch, ss in magic ring.

Round 2: 1ch, turn, 2dc in ch sp, working in back loop only: (2dc in next st, 2htr in next st, 2tr in next 2 sts, 2htr in next st, 2dc in next st), 2dc in 2ch sp, 1ch, ss in magic ring.

Round 3: 1ch, turn, 1dc in next 3 sts, working in back loop only: (1htr in next 10 sts), 1dc in last 3 sts, 1ch, ss in magic ring.

Round 4: 1ch, turn, 1dc in next 3 sts, 1dc in sp between dc and htr, 1dc in next sp between sts, 2dc in next sp between sts, [1dc in next sp between sts] twice, 2dc in next sp between sts, [1dc in next sp between sts] twice, 2dc in next sp between sts, [1dc in next sp between sts] twice, 1dc in next 3 sts, 1ch, ss in magic ring.

Round 5: Do not turn work, 1back-dc (crab st) in every st, ss in magic ring to finish.

CLASSIC FISH

Materials

- 0.5mm (12 steel) crochet hook
- DMC Fil à Dentelles in Yellow 726
- Embroidery needle

Finished size

18mm x 15mm (¾in x ⅝in)

Round 1: Make a magic ring, into ring work 6dc, do not join, but work in a spiral throughout.

Round 2: [2dc in next st] twice, 2htr in next st, [2tr in next st] twice, 2htr in next st, [2dc in next st] twice.

Round 3: 1dc in the next 6 sts, 2tr in the next 4 sts, 1dc in next 6 sts.

Round 4: (1dc, 3ch, 1dc) in next st (makes top of mouth), 1dc in next 3 sts, 2ch, 2tr in same st, 2ch, 2tr in next st, 1dc in next 4 sts, (ss, 3ch, 3dtr, 2ch, 1dtr, 3ch, ss) in next st, (ss, 2ch, 3tr, 2ch, 1tr, 2ch, ss) in next st, 1dc in next 4 sts, (1htr, 2ch, 3tr) in next st, 1dc in next 3 sts, (1dc, 3ch, ss) in last st (makes bottom of mouth).

SAND DOLLAR

Materials

- 0.75mm (14/10 steel) crochet hook
- Gütermann top stitching thread in Ecru 169
- Embroidery needle

Finished size

18mm x 18mm (¾in x ¾in)

Round 1: Make a magic ring, into ring work 3ch (counts as 1tr), 14tr, ss in first tr.

Round 2: 1ch, 1dc in same st, *2FPtr in next st, 1dc in next 2 sts, rep from * 4 times omitting last dc, ss in first dc.

Round 3: 1ch, 2dc in first dc, *2FPtr in round 2 Fptrs together, 2dc in next 2 sts, rep from * 4 times omitting last 2 dc, ss in first dc.

Round 4: 1ch, 1dc in next 3 sts, *4ch, 1dc in next 6 sts, rep from * 4 times omitting last 3 dc, ss in first dc.

Round 5: 3ch (counts as 1tr), 1tr in next 2 sts, *3dc in 4ch sp, 1tr in next 6 sts, rep from * 4 times omitting last 3 tr, ss in first tr.

Round 6: 1back-dc (crab st) in every st.

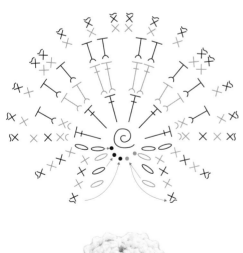

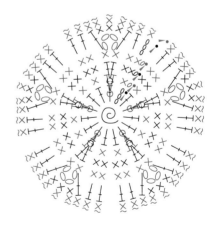

BOAT

Materials

- 0.75mm (14/10 steel) crochet hook
- Gütermann top stitching thread, colours used in this order: Mustard 412, Mid Red 46, Cream 414, Mid Blue 965
- Embroidery needle

Finished size

20mm x 27mm (¾in x 1in)

Base

Make 7ch.

Row 1: 2dc in second ch from hook, 1dc in next 4 ch, 2dc in last ch (8 sts).

Row 2: 1ch, turn, 2dc in first st, 1dc in every st to last st, 2dc in last st (10 sts).

Row 3: As row 3 (12 sts).

Rows 4 and 5: 1ch, turn, 1dc in every st.

Row 6: Change colour, ss in front loop of first st, (1ch, ss in front loop) in every st.

Sail

Row 7: Change colour, working in back loops only: ss in second st of row 5, 1ch, 1dc in same st, 1dc in next 9 sts (10 sts).

Row 8: 1ch, turn, dc2tog, 1dc in every st to end (9 sts).

Row 9: 1ch, turn, dc2tog, 1dc in every st to last 2 sts, dc2tog (7 sts).

Rows 10 and 11: As rows 8 and 9 (4 sts).

Row 12: As row 8 (3 sts).

Row 13: 1ch, turn, dctog over first 2 sts, dc2tog over same st and last st (2 sts).

Row 14: 1ch, dc2tog, ss to finish (1 st).

Mast and Flag

Worked using surface crochet, using Blue ss on row 7 in the fourth st front loop only, ss in each st working up the sail to the top.

Row 1: 4ch, starting in second ch from hook, 1dc in next 3 ch (3 sts).

Row 2: 1ch, turn, dc2tog, 1dc in last st (2 sts).

Row 3: 1ch, turn, dc2tog (1 st).

Row 4: 1ch, turn, 1dc, ss to finish.

Rubber Ring

Round 1: Using Cream, make a magic ring, into ring work *3dc (changing to Red on last st), 3dc (changing to Cream on last st), rep from * once more, ss in first dc.

MANTA RAY

Materials

- 0.75mm (14/10 steel) crochet hook
- Gütermann top stitching thread, colours used: Lilac 158; **Amigurumi version**: White 800; **Eyes**: Purple 810
- Embroidery needle
- Small amount of stuffing if making Amigurumi version

Finished size

30mm x 25mm (1⅛in x 1in)

Row 1: Using Lilac, 5ch, starting at second ch from hook, 1dc in every ch (4 sts).

Row 2: 1ch, turn, 2dc in first st, 1dc in every st to last st, 2dc in last st (6 sts).

Rows 3 to 5: As round 2 (12 sts).

Row 6: 1ch, turn, 2dc in first st, 1dc in next 4 sts, 2tr in next 2 sts, 1dc in next 4 sts, 2dc in last st.

Row 7: 1ch, turn, 2dc in first st, 1dc in next 4 sts, 3tr in next st, skip 1 st, 3tr in next 2 sts, skip 1 st, 3tr in next st, 1dc in next 4 sts, 2dc in last st.

Row 8: 1ch, turn, 2dc in first st, 1dc in next 11 sts, 6ch, starting in second ch from hook, 1dc in next 5 sts, (makes tail), 1dc in next 11 sts, 2dc in in last st.

Row 9: 2ch (makes fin tip), 1dc in each row down side of fin, 3ch, starting at second ch from hook, 1dc in next 2 chs, 4dc in the 4ch sp of row 1, 3ch, starting at second ch from hook, 1dc in next 2 chs, 1dc in each row up other side of wing to row 8, 1ch, htr in beg st of row 9.

To make an amigurumi manta ray, make another body in White and embroider a little mouth and gills in Lilac. Place the two pieces together wrong sides facing each other. Join by whip stitching the back loops of the outer rows together. Add a small amount of stuffing before sewing together.

Using Purple embroider eyes.

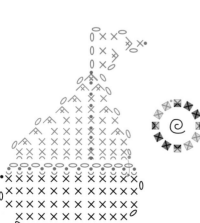

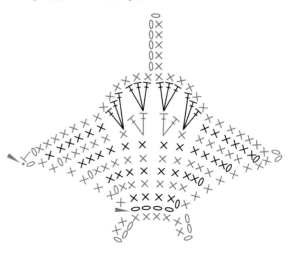

Clam shell pendant

A tiny pendant for tiny sea treasures. This is a great project for hidden glitz and locket lovers. Who doesn't love a pendant that opens and closes?

Materials

- 0.75mm (14/10 steel) crochet hook
- Gütermann top stitching thread, colours used: Light Blue 143, Fawn 722
- A selection of pearl beads and seed beads
- Fine sewing cotton for sewing the beads
- Sewing Needle
- Scissors
- Flat nose pliers
- 6mm open jump ring, either round or oval shaped

Finished size

16mm (½in) x 16mm (½in) x 10mm (½in)

Liner

Row 1: Using Light Blue make a magic ring, into ring work 6dc, do not ss to join.

Row 2: Working in a spiral, 2dc in next st, 2htr in next 4 sts, 2dc in last st.

Row 3: 1dc in next 3 sts, 2htr in next 6 sts, 1dc in rem 3 sts, ss in beg st to finish.

Crochet two Clam Shells in Fawn and and two liners in Light Blue.

Sew the liner inside the shell by whip stitching the back loops of the last round of the liner to the underneath the edging of the shell **(1)**.

Sew a cluster of beads to inside of one of the clam shells. Traditionally there should only be one pearl but you can sew as many as you like! **(2)**.

Sew the top of the clam shells together using a few blanket stitches **(3)**.

Use the blanket stitches as an anchor to crochet a short row of (ss, 1ch) in each st along the top of the shell **(4)**.

Use pliers to attach the jump ring to the top of the clam shell, threading it through the magic ring so that it is centralised **(5)**.

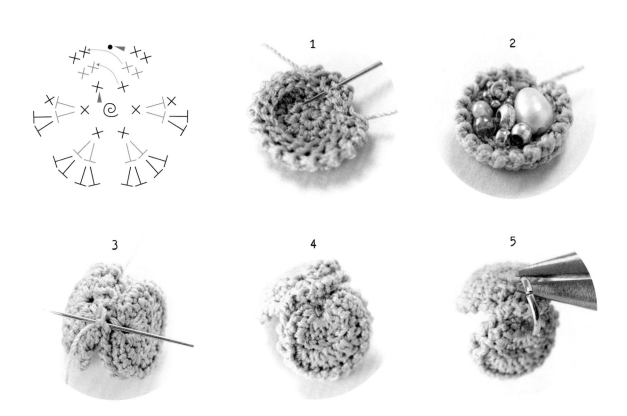

Occasions

There is nothing like being able to celebrate a favourite
occasion or event by making things in crochet. Whether they be
for gifts, decoration, jewellery or a treat for yourself, these
little motifs are great for adding to the fun and festivities.
All the motifs are worked with Gütermann hand quilting cotton
with a 0.5mm or 0.6mm (12 steel) hook.

HOLLY LEAF

Materials

- 0.5mm-0.6mm (12 steel) crochet hook
- Gütermann hand quilting cotton in Emerald Green 8244
- Embroidery needle

Finished size

30mm x 15mm (1⅛in x ⅝in)

Round 1: Make a magic ring, 3ch, 1tr in magic ring and pull ring tight to make first loop, (3ch, 1tr) in ch sp to make second loop, repeat to make a row of 5 loops.

Round 2: 3ch, (counts as 1tr), (2tr, 2ch, 3tr) in first loop, skip second loop, (3dtr, 2ch, 3dtr) in third loop, skip fourth loop, (3tr, 2ch, 3tr) in fifth loop, 3ch (makes point on end of leaf), rotate work and continue on the other side of the loops, (3tr, 2ch, 3tr) in fifth loop, skip fourth loop, (3dtr, 2ch, 3dtr) in third loop, skip second loop, (3tr, 2ch, 3tr) in first loop, 1ch, 1tr in beg 3ch.

Round 3: 1ch, 2dc in side of tr, 1dc between every st around the leaf, with (1dc, 2ch, 1dc) in every 2ch sp and (2dc, 3ch, 2dc) in the 3ch sp at bottom of leaf, in last 1ch sp work 2dc, 3ch, ss in beg 1ch.

SNOWFLAKE

Materials

- 0.5mm-0.6mm (12 steel) crochet hook
- Gütermann hand quilting cotton in Light Ivory 919
- Embroidery needle

Finished size

20mm x 20mm (¾in x ¾in)

Starching is highly recommended, but if you would rather not, this pattern makes a beautiful lacy flower.

Round 1: Make a magic ring, into ring work 3ch (counts as tr), tr2tog, [4ch, tr3tog] 5 times, 4ch, ss in beg 3ch.

Round 2: *(Ss into next 4ch sp, 4ch, 1tr, 3ch, ss in tr (makes picot), 1tr, 4ch, ss in fourth ch from hook, 1ch, 2tr, 3ch picot in second tr, 4ch, ss) in same 4ch sp, rep from * 5 times.

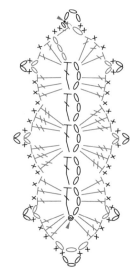

74

DANISH HEART

Materials

- 0.5mm–0.6mm (12 steel) crochet hook
- Gütermann hand quilting cotton, colours used: Light Ivory 919, Lime Green 9837
- Embroidery needle

Finished size

25mm x 23mm (1in x ⅞in)

Make one of the following shape in each colour.

Round 1: Make a magic ring, into ring work 3ch, 1tr, close magic ring (makes 1 loop), 3ch, 1tr in loop sp (makes 2 loops), continue until you have 12 loops.

Round 2: 2ch (does not count as htr), 3htr in next 11 loops, 9htr in twelfth loop, 3htr in next 10 loops on other side, 6htr in beg loop, ss in first htr to finish.

Round 3: 1ch, 1dc in first htr, 1dc in next 2 sts, 30ch, skip 30 sts, 1dc in next 3 sts, 2dc in next 3 sts, 1dc in next 3 sts, 30ch, skip 30 sts, 1dc in next 3 sts, 2dc in next 3 sts, ss in first dc.

Round 4: 2ch, 1htr in next 3 dc, 30htr in 30ch sp, 1htr in next 3 sts, 2htr in next 6 sts, 1htr in next 3 sts, 30htr in 30ch sp, 1htr in the next 3 sts, 2htr in next 6 sts, ss in first htr.

Round 5: 1ch, 1dc in every st, ss in first dc.

Round 6: (Skip 1 st, 1back-dc (crab st) in next st), last st should land on beg st of round 5, ss in first dc to finish.

Weave both shapes together to form heart shape.

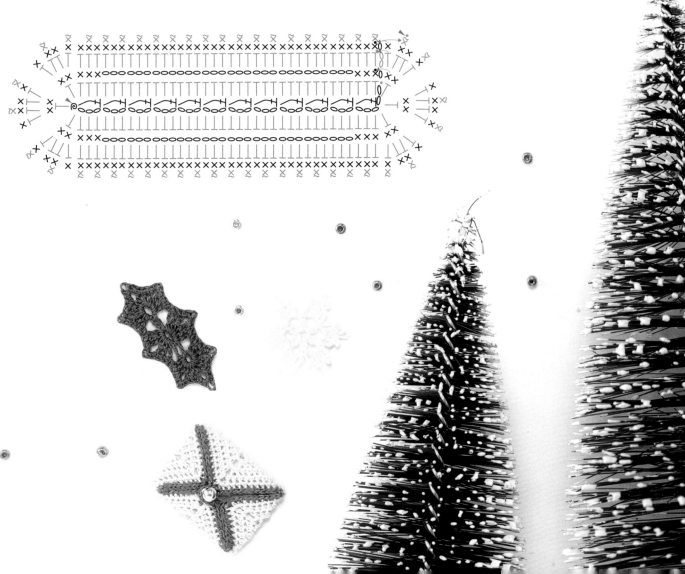

INVITATION ENVELOPE

Materials

- 0.5mm–0.6mm (12 steel) crochet hook
- Gütermann hand quilting cotton, colours used: **Main section**: Light Ivory 919; **Border and embroidery**: Mid Blue 5725, Mid Red 1974
- Embroidery needle
- Small bead

Finished size

25mm x 25mm (1in x 1in)

Round 1: Make a magic ring, into ring work 2ch (counts as 1htr), 3htr, [2ch, 4htr] 3 times, 1ch, 1dc in beg 2ch (hook is now positioned on the tip of the corner).

Round 2: 2ch (counts as htr), *1htr in every st to 2ch sp, (1htr, 2ch, 1hr) in 2ch corner sp, rep from * 3 times omitting last ch and htr, 1dc in beg 2ch (6 htr per side).

Round 3: As round 2 (8 htr per side).

Round 4: As round 2 (10 htr per side).

Round 5: As round 2 (12 htr per side).

Round 6: As round 2 (14 htr per side).

Round 7: As round 2 (16 htr per side).

Round 8: As round 2 (18 htr per side).

Round 9: 1ch, work as for round 2 using dc sts instead of htr sts (20 dc per side).

Round 10: Change colour, ss in 2ch corner sp, 1ch, 1dc in same sp (changing colour on last yarn over pull through), *1dc in next st, 1dc (changing colour on last yarn over pull through) in next st, rep from * to corner ch sp, 2dc in corner 2ch sp changing colours as before, continue in the same way around rest of square, except work (1dc, 8ch, 1dc) in one of the corners for a buttonhole, ss in beg dc to finish.

Fold the square corner to corner, whip stitch the back loops of three of the edges together. Sew a bead to the front of the envelope and embroider a stamp and address on the back.

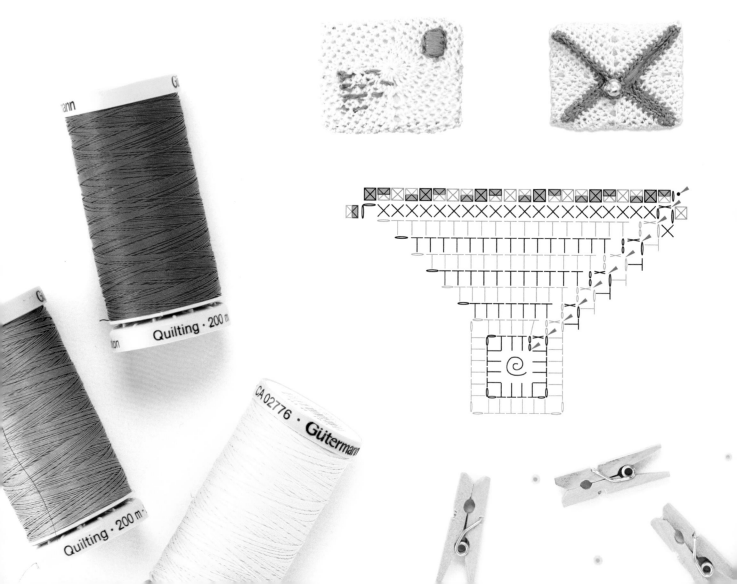

GRANNY HEART

Materials

- 0.5mm-0.6mm (12 steel) crochet hook
- Gütermann hand quilting cotton, colours used in this order: Turquoise 6934, Light Ivory 919, Sage Green 8816
- Embroidery needle

Finished size

15mm x 15mm (⅝in x ⅝in)

Round 1: Make a magic ring, into ring work 3ch (counts as 1tr), 2tr, 2ch, [3tr, 2ch] 3 times, ss in beg 3ch to finish.

Round 2: Change colour, ss in round 1 first corner ch sp, 4ch, 5tr in same ch sp, 1ch, 3htr in next ch sp, 2ch, 3htr in next ch sp, 1ch, (5tr, 4ch, ss) in last ch sp, 2ch, ss in first corner ch sp.

Round 3: 1ch, 5dc in 4ch sp, 2dc in the next 4 sps between sts, 2dc in 1ch sp, 1dc in next 3 sts, (2htr, 2ch, 2htr) in 2ch sp (makes heart point), 1dc in next 3 sts, 2dc in 1ch sp, 2dc in next 4 sps between sts, 5dc in last ch sp, 1ch, ss in corner 2ch sp to finish.

Round 4: Change colour, ss in 2ch sp from round 2 at top of heart, 1ch, 1dc in next 20 sts, (2dc, 2ch, 2dc) in heart tip ch sp, 1dc in next 20 sts, 1ch, ss in beg 2ch sp from round 2 to finish. Trim ends and sew in to finish.

LACE HEART

Materials

- 0.5mm-0.6mm (12 steel) crochet hook
- Gütermann hand quilting cotton in Royal Blue 5133
- Embroidery needle

Finished size

10mm x 10mm (⅜in x ⅜in)

Round 1: Make a magic ring, into ring work 5ch, 1tr, [4ch, 1dtr] twice, 4ch, 1tr, 5ch, ss in magic ring, draw magic ring to a close but not too tight. Use thread end to tie one knot through magic ring to stop it from coming undone.

Round 2: Turn work over, crochet over thread end as you work round 2, 1ch, 5dc in ch sp, 4dc in next ch sp, (2dc, 2ch, 2dc) in next ch sp (centre bottom), 4dc in next ch sp, 5dc in last ch sp, 1ch, ss in magic ring.

Round 3: Do not turn work over, working backwards, 1back-dc (crab st) in next 11 sts, turn work over, (1dc, 2ch, 1dc) in heart point ch sp, turn work back over, 1back-dc in next 11 sts until magic ring is reached, ss in magic ring to finish. Trim ends and sew in to finish.

Round 3 alternative: Instead of working backwards with back-dc, turn work over and work forwards, replacing 1back-dc with (1ss, 1ch) for a textured edge.

BAT

Materials

- 0.5mm-0.6mm (12 steel) crochet hook
- Gütermann hand quilting cotton in Dark Grey 5114
- Embroidery needle

Finished size

30mm x 10mm (1⅛in x ⅜in)

Round 1: Make a magic ring, into ring work 3ch, 1tr in magic ring, close magic ring (makes 1 loop), 3ch, 1tr in loop space (makes 2 loops), continue until you have 7 loops.

Round 2: 3ch, (1tr, 1dtr, 2ch, 1dtr, 1tr, 1htr) in first loop sp, (1htr, 1tr, 1dtr, 2ch, 1dtr, 1tr, 1htr) in second loop sp, (1htr, 1tr, 2ch, 1tr, 1htr) in third loop sp, (1ch, 2dc, 1ch) in fourth loop sp, (1htr, 1tr, 2ch, 1tr, 1htr) in fifth loop sp, (1htr, 1tr, 1dtr, 2ch, 1dtr, 1tr, 1htr) in sixth loop sp, (1htr, 1tr, 1dtr, 2ch, 1dtr, 1tr, 3ch, ss) in seventh loop sp, continuing on other side of loops, (1ch, 2dc) in seventh loop sp, 3dc in sixth loop sp, 2dc in fifth loop sp, (ss, 3ch, 2dc, 3ch, ss) in fourth loop sp, 2dc in third loop sp, 3dc in second loop sp, 2dc in first loop sp.

Round 3: (3dc, 2ch, 1dc) in beg 3ch loop of round 2, 1dc in next 2 sts, (1dc, 1htr, 2ch, 1htr, 1dc) in 2ch sp, 1dc in next 6 sts, (1dc, 1htr, 2ch, 1htr, 1dc) in 2ch sp, 1dc in next 5 sts, (1dc, 2ch, 1dc) in next 2ch sp, 1dc in next 2 sts, 1ch, ss in next 2 sts, 1ch, 1dc in next 2 sts, (1dc, 2ch, 1dc) in the next 2ch sp, 1dc in next 5 sts, (1dc, 1htr, 2ch, 1htr, 1dc) in next 2ch sp, 1dc in the next 6 sts, (1dc, 1htr, 2ch, 1htr, 1dc) in next 2ch sp, 1dc in last 2 sts, (1dc, 2ch, 3dc) in 3ch sp, ss in 1ch of round 2 to finish.

PUMPKIN

Materials

- 0.5mm-0.6mm (12 steel) crochet hook
- Gütermann hand quilting cotton, colours used: Orange 2045, Dark Green 8113
- Embroidery needle

Finished size

13mm x 10mm (½in x ⅜in)

Round 1: Using Orange make a magic ring, into ring work 2ch, 11htr, 2ch, ss.

Round 2: 3ch, 3tr in first st, 2tr In the next 4 sts, 1ss in the next 2 sps between sts, 2tr in next 4 sts, 3tr in last st, 3ch, ss in magic ring.

Round 3: 1ch, 3dc in 3ch sp, 2dc in next 3 sts, 1dc in next 8 sts, 1ss in next 2 sps between sts from round 1, 1dc in next 8 sts, 2dc in last 3 sts, 3dc in 3ch sp, 1ch, ss in magic ring.

Using Dark Green ss in magic ring, 3ch, 1tr in magic ring, 3ch, ss in magic ring.

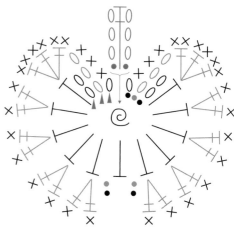

SKULL

Materials

- 0.5mm-0.6mm (12 steel) crochet hook
- Gütermann hand quilting cotton in Orange 2045
- Embroidery needle

Finished size

13mm x 15mm (½in x ⅝in)

Round 1: Make a magic ring, into ring work 10ch, 8dtr, 7ch, 1tr, 3ch, 1dc into beg 10ch sp.

Round 2: 7dc into same ch sp (makes 8dc in total), 2htr in next 7 sps between sts, 8dc into 7ch sp, 3ch, [1tr, 1ch] 3 times in 3ch sp, 3ch, ss in last dc st of round 1.

Round 3: (1ch, ss) into next 29 sts, 4ch, 1tr in 3ch sp, 1ch, (1tr, 1ch) in next 2 1ch sp, 1ch, 1tr in next 3ch sp (makes lower jaw), 4ch, ss into last dc of round 1 to finish.

EGG

Materials

- 0.5mm-0.6mm (12 steel) crochet hook
- Gütermann hand quilting cotton in Yellow 758
- Embroidery needle

Finished size

12mm x 10mm (½in x ⅜in)

Round 1: Make a magic ring, into ring work 5ch, 2ttr, 2dtr, 9tr, 2dtr, 2ttr, ss in fifth ch.

Round 2: 1ch, 1dc in next 4 sts, 2dc in next 9 sts, 1dc in last 4 sts, ss in beg ch.

Round 3: (1ch, 1ss) in every st, ss in first ch sp of round 2.

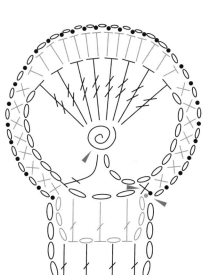

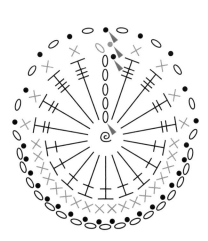

Danish heart mini pendant

This Danish heart is traditionally made from paper for Christmas decorations and gift food packaging. Though usually red and white, the design can be worn all year round by using different colours. The pattern starts with a series of loops rather than a row of chain stitches. These are not just for decorative purposes but are there to make the foundation row easier to hold while crocheting the stitches into it.

Materials

- 0.75mm (14/10 steel) crochet hook
- Gütermann top stitching thread in two colours of your choice
- Beading embroidery needle
- 3mm bead
- Pendant chain

25mm x 23mm (1in x 1in)

Begin by making two pieces of the motif as described earlier in this chapter. Crochet the little fastening strap separately, it starts in a similar way to the first 2 rounds of the heart motif.

Crochet the fastening strap

Round 1: Make a magic ring, into ring work 3ch, 1tr, (makes first loop), 3ch, 1tr in loop space (makes two loops), continue until a total of 8 loops have been made, 4ch, 1dtr in last loop sp to make button hole.

Round 2: 2ch (counts as 1htr), 3htr in same loop, 3htr in the next 7 loop sps, 9htr in the last loop, 3htr in the next 7 loops on the other side of the band, 7htr in the buttonhole loop, ss in beg 2 ch sp.

Round 3: (1back-dc, skip 1 st) all around the strap, ss in first back-dc to finish.

Fold the two halves of the heart and weave together **(1)**.

Use excess thread to sew and secure the weaving in place. Sew further up the sides to make the bag more secure **(2)**.

On the back of the heart, place the end of the strap without the button hole between the two halves where they overlap and sew neatly in place **(3)**.

Sew bead to the front of the heart and then fasten the button hole over it. When fastened, the chain can be threaded underneath the strap **(4)**.

Thread the pendant chain through the loop of the strap.

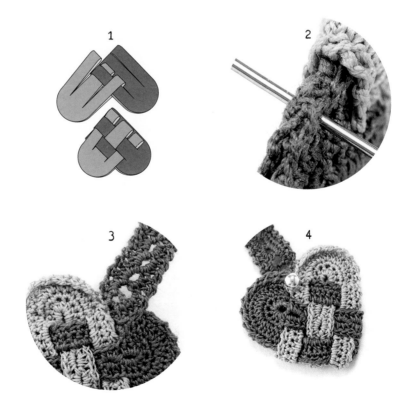

Mandalas

Whether they are drawn, painted or crocheted, mandalas
are extremely satisfying to make. Traditionally used as a
means of prayer and meditation across many cultures, they
invoke focus and relaxation through the repetitive nature of
their patterns. Place them in a frame, stretch them over an
embroidery hoop, or create home décor pieces with a larger
hook and yarn. All the motifs are worked with Gütermann hand
quilting cotton with a 0.6mm (12 steel) hook.

SARAH

Materials

- 0.6mm (12 steel) crochet hook
- Gütermann hand quilting cotton, colours used in this order: Mid Red 1974, Black 5201, Light Ivory 919, Lime Green 9837, Black (again), Dark Red 2833, Mid Red (again), Black (again)
- Embroidery needle

Finished size

40mm x 40mm (1½in x 1½in)

Round 1: Make a magic ring, 4ch (counts as 1tr, 1ch), [1tr, 1ch] 15 times into ring, ss in first tr to finish.

Round 2: Change colour, 1dc in any ch sp, *(2tr, 1dtr, 2ch, 1dtr, 2tr) in next ch sp, 1dc in next ch sp, rep from * 7 times, omitting last dc, ss in first dc to finish (8 petals).

Round 3: Change colour, ss in any 2ch sp, 4ch (counts as 1dtr), 6dtr in same ch sp, 1ch, (7dtr, 1ch) in each 2ch sp around, ss in beg 4ch sp to finish.

Round 4: Change colour, 1dc in 1ch sp, *1dc in next 7 sts, (1dc, 4ch, 1dc) in next ch sp, rep from * 7 times omitting last dc, ss in first dc to finish.

Round 5: Change colour, 1dc in fifth st from a 4ch sp (centre tr in a group), *8dtr in next 4ch sp, 1dc in centre tr in next group, rep from * 7 times, omitting last dc, ss in first dc to finish.

Round 6: Change colour, *2dc in third, fourth and fifth sps between dtr sts in a group, 1ch, 2dtr in 2 sps between end dtr's of 2 groups from round 5 and dc's from round 4, 1ch, rep from * 7 times, ss in first dc to finish.

Round 7: Change colour, 1dc in 1ch sp at beg of last round, 1dc in every st and (1dc, 4ch, 1dc) in every 1ch sp, 1dc in beg ch sp, 4ch, ss in beg dc to finish.

KIRSTY

Materials

- 0.6mm (12 steel) crochet hook
- Gütermann hand quilting cotton, colours used in this order: Mustard Yellow 956, Yellow 758, Light Lilac 4226, Lilac 4434, Dark Purple 3832
- Embroidery needle

Finished size

35mm x 35mm (1⅜in x 1⅜in)

Round 1: Make a magic ring, 5ch (counts as 1tr, 2ch), [1tr, 2ch] 9 times in ring, ss in third ch of 5ch to finish.

Round 2: Change colour, 3ch (counts as 1tr) in 2ch sp, tr3tog in same ch sp, 4ch, (tr4tog, 4ch) in every 2ch sp, ss in beg tr3tog to finish (10 petals).

Round 3: Change colour, ss in 4ch sp, *4ch, 3dtr in same ch sp, 1ch, 3dtr in next ch sp, 4ch, ss in same ch sp, 4ch, ss in next ch sp, rep from * 4 times (5 petals).

Round 4: Change colour, ss in 4ch sp between petals, *4ch, 2tr in next 4ch sp, 2tr in next 2 sps between sts, (1tr, 2ch, 1tr) in 1ch sp, 2tr in next 2 sps between sts, 2tr in next 4ch sp, 4ch, ss in next 4ch sp, rep from * 4 times.

Round 5: Change colour, starting in first tr in round 4, *1dc in next 7 tr, (1htr, 2ch, 1htr) in 2ch sp, 1dc in next 7 tr, 2ch, 2dtr in next 2 4ch sps, 2ch, rep from * 4 times, ss in first dc to finish.

Round 6: Starting in first dc of round 5, *1dc in next 8 sts, (1dc, 2ch, 1dc) in 2ch sp, 1dc in next 8 sts, 3ch, 2tr between first and second dtr, (1dtr, 3ch, 1dtr) between second and third dtr, 2tr between third and fourth dtr, 3ch, rep from * 4 times, ss in first dc to finish.

MATTEA

Materials

- 0.6mm (12 steel) crochet hook
- Gütermann hand quilting cotton, colours used in this order: Dark Purple 3832, Turquoise 6934, Bright Red 1974, Orange 2045, Yellow 758, Pink 2955, Sage Green 8816
- Embroidery needle

Finished size

20mm x 20mm (¾in x ¾in)

Round 1: Make a magic ring, [1dc, 2ch] 6 times into ring, ss in ring to finish.

Round 2: Change colour, 2ch in 2ch sp, 1htr in same sp, (2htr, 2ch, 2htr) in next 5 ch sps, 2htr in beg ch sp, 2ch, ss in beg 2ch to finish.

Round 3: Change colour, ss in 2ch sp, 4ch (does not count as 1dtr), 7dtr in same ch sp, 7dtr in next 5 ch sps, ss in beg ch sp to finish.

Round 4: Change colour, 1dc in fourth (central) dtr in a group, 1dc in next 3 sts, *1 elongated dc between second and third htr in the group of 4 below from round 2, 1dc in next 7 sts, rep from * 5 times omitting last 4 dc, ss in first dc to finish.

Round 5: Change colour, start at beg st of last round, 1dc in every st, ss to finish.

Round 6: Change colour, start at beg st of last round, 1back-dc (crab st) in every st, ss to finish.

Round 7: Change colour, working sts into round 5 (going over round 6), ss into first dc of round 5, 1back-dc, (1ch, skip 1 st, 1back-dc) to end, ss in beg ss to finish.

CAROLINE

Materials

- 0.6mm (12 steel) crochet hook
- Gütermann hand quilting cotton, colours used in this order: Turquoise 6934, Light Green 9837, Pink 2955, Yellow 758, Orange 2045, White 5709
- Embroidery needle

Finished size

27mm x 27mm (1in x 1in)

Round 1: Make a magic ring, into ring work 3ch (counts as 1tr), tr3tog, 3ch, [tr4tog, 3ch] 6 times, ss in beg tr3tog to finish.

Round 2: Change colour, (ss, 2ch, 4tr, 2ch ss, 2ch) in every 3ch sp, ss in beg ss to finish.

Round 3: Change colour, *(1dc, 2ch, 1dc) between second and third tr in a 4tr group, skip ch2 sp, 3tr in next 2ch sp, skip ch2 sp, rep from * 6 times, ss in first dc to finish.

Round 4: Change colour, *(1dc, 3ch, 1dc) in 2ch sp, (4tr, 2ch, 4tr) in middle tr of 3tr group, rep from * 6 times, ss in first dc to finish.

Round 5: Change colour, *(1dc, 3ch, 1dc) in 2ch sp, 7tr in 3ch sp, rep from * 6 times, ss in first dc to finish.

Round 6: Change colour, *(1dc, 3ch, 1dc) in 3ch sp, 1dc in next 4 sts, (1dc, 3ch, 1dc) in next st, 1dc in next 4 sts, rep from * 6 times, ss in first dc to finish.

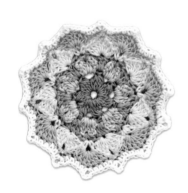

DENISE

Materials

- 0.6mm (12 steel) crochet hook

- Gütermann hand quilting cotton, colours used in this order: Light Green 9837, Dark Green 8113, Orange 2045, Bright Red 1974, Mid Green 8724, Light Green 9837 (again), Ivory 919, Bright Red 1974 (again), Dark Green 8113 (again), Orange 2045 (again)

- Embroidery needle

Finished size

35mm x 35mm (1⅜in x 1⅜in)

Round 1: Make a magic ring, 8dc in ring, ss in first dc to finish.

Round 2: Change colour, 6ch, (1tr, 3ch) in each st, ss in third ch of beg 6ch sp to finish.

Round 3: Change colour, 2ch in 3ch sp (counts as 1htr) 2htr in same sp, 1ch, (3htr, 1ch) in next 7 3ch sps, ss in beg 2ch to finish.

Round 4: Change colour, 4ch in 1ch sp (counts as 1tr, 1ch), 1tr in same sp, 4ch, (1tr, 1ch, 1tr, 4ch) in next 7 1ch sps, ss in beg 4ch sp to finish.

Round 5: Change colour, (4ch, 1htr) in beg 4ch sp, *(2ch, 1htr, 2ch) in next 4ch sp, (1htr, 1ch, 1htr) in 1ch sp, rep from * 7 times, omitting last (1htr, 1ch, 1htr), ss in beg 4ch sp to finish.

Round 6: Change colour, (4ch, 1htr) in beg 4ch sp, *(2ch, 1htr) in next 2ch sp, (1htr, 2ch) in next 2ch sp, (1htr, 1ch, 1htr) in 1ch sp, rep from * 7 times omitting last (1htr, 1ch, 1htr), ss in beg 4ch sp to finish.

Round 7: Change colour, (4ch, 1htr) in beg 4ch sp, *(2ch, 1htr) in next 2ch sp, 1htr in sp between next 2 htr, (1htr, 2ch) in next 2ch sp, (1htr, 1ch, 1htr) in 1ch sp, rep from * 7 times omitting last (1htr, 1ch, 1htr), ss in beg 4ch sp to finish.

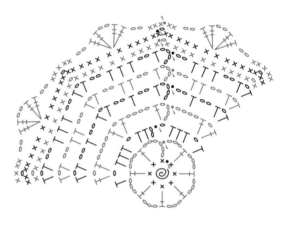

Round 8: Change colour, 1dc in beg 4ch sp, *3dc in 2ch sp, 1dc in next 2 sps between sts, 3dc in next 2ch sp, (1dc, 1ch, 1dc) in 1ch sp, rep from * 7 times omitting last dc, ss in beg dc to finish.

Round 9: Change colour, starting in 1ch sp, 1dc in every st and (1dc, 1ch, 1dc) in every 1ch sp.

Round 10: Change colour, dc in 1ch sp, 1dc in next 2 sts, *2ch, skip 4 sts, (2dtr, 2ch, 2dtr) in sp before next st, 2ch, skip 4 sts, 1dc in next 2 sts, 1dc in 1ch sp, 1dc in next 2 sts, rep from * 7 times omitting last 3 dc, ss in first dc to finish.

MOIRA

Materials

- 0.6mm (12 steel) crochet hook
- Gütermann hand quilting cotton, colours used in this order: Bright Red 1974, Dark Red 2833, Orange 2045, Light Ivory 919, Light Green 9837, Mid Green 8724, Dark Green 8113
- Embroidery needle

Finished size

35mm x 35mm (1⅜in x 1⅜in)

Round 1: Make a magic ring, 4ch, [1dtr, 1ch] 3 times, [1tr, 1ch] 3 times, [1ch, 1tr] 3 times, [1ch, 1dtr] 3 times, 4ch, ss in magic ring.

Round 2: 1ch, turn work, 5dc in 4ch sp, 2dc in next 5 ch sps, (1dc, 2ch, 1dc) in next ch sp (heart tip), 2dc in next 5 ch sps, 5dc in 4ch sp, 1ch, ss in magic ring.

Round 3: Change colour, ss in magic ring, 1ch, 1dc in next 16 sts, (1dc, 3ch, 1dc) in heart tip ch sp, 1dc in next 16 sts, 1ch, ss in magic ring to finish.

Round 4: Change colour, ss in third dc of round 3, 3ch (counts as 1tr), 2tr in same st, 4ch, skip 3 sts, 3tr in next st, 4ch, skip 3 sts, 3dtr in next st, 4ch, 6dtr in heart tip ch sp, 4ch, skip 6 sts, 3dtr in next st, [4ch, skip 3 sts, 3tr in next st] twice, 4ch, ss in beg 3ch to finish.

Round 5: Change colour, ss in last 4ch sp at top of heart, 2ch (counts as htr), 2htr in same sp, *[1htr in sp between next 2 sts] twice, 6htr in 4ch sp, rep from * 6 times omitting last 3 htr, ss in beg 2ch to finish.

Round 6: 1dc in first htr, 1dc in every st, ss in first dc to finish.

Round 7: Change colour, starting at beg 1dc of round 6, 2ch (counts as 1htr), 1htr in same st, 1ch, *skip 1 st, 2htr in next st, 1ch, rep from * to end, ss in beg 2ch to finish. There may not be a stitch to skip from round 6 at the end but still work the last pair of htr and 1ch.

Round 8: Change colour, ss in last ch sp above heart, *5tr in next sp (makes shell st), ss in next ch sp, rep from * 14 times, with last ss in beg ch sp to finish.

Round 9: Change colour, ss in same round 7 ch sp as last round, 5ch, *working in back loop only, 5tr in third tr in next group (centre of shell), 1ch, 1dtr in round 7 ch sp directly below, 1ch, rep from * 14 times omitting last dtr, ss in fourth ch of beg 5ch sp to finish.

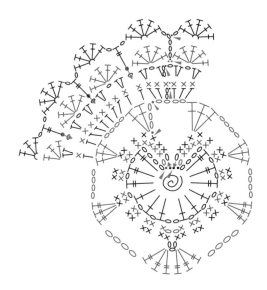

KATE

Materials

- 0.6mm (12 steel) crochet hook
- Gütermann hand quilting cotton, colours used in this order: Dark Red 2833, Mid Green 8724, Light Green 9837, Bright Red 1974, Light Ivory 919, Orange 2045, Black 5201
- Embroidery needle

Finished size

25mm x 25mm (1in x 1in)

Round 1: Make a magic ring, 12dc in ring, ss in first dc to finish.

Round 2: Change colour, 3ch (counts as 1tr), 1tr in same st, 2tr in every st, ss in beg 3ch to finish (24 sts).

Round 3: Change colour, 3ch (counts as 1tr), tr2tog in same st, 3ch, tr3tog in same st, 3ch, *skip 3 sts, (tr3tog, 3ch, tr3tog) in next st, 3ch, rep from * 4 times, ss in beg tr2tog to finish (6 leaves).

Round 4: Change colour, ss in 3ch sp between pair of leaves, 3ch (counts as 1tr), (tr2tog, 2ch, 5trpop, 2ch, tr3tog) in same sp, 4ch, *(tr3tog, 2ch, 5trpop, 2ch, tr3tog, 4ch) in next ch sp, skip next ch sp, rep from * 4 times, ss in beg tr2tog to finish.

Round 5: Change colour, *3dc in next two 2ch sps, 4dtr in round 3 3ch sp directly beneath, rep from * 5 times, ss in first dc to finish.

Round 6: Change colour, 1dc in every st.

Round 7: Change colour, *1back-dc (crab st), skip 1 st, rep from * to end, ss in first st to finish.

ROSA

Materials

- 0.6mm (12 steel) crochet hook
- Gütermann hand quilting cotton, colours used in this order: Dark Blue 5322, Royal Blue 5133, Mid Blue 5725, Light Blue 5217, White 5709
- Embroidery needle

Finished size

25mm x 25mm (1in x 1in)

Round 1: Make a magic ring, 3ch (counts as 1tr), 1tr in ring, 3ch, [2tr, 3ch] 5 times, ss in beg 3ch to finish.

Round 2: Change colour, ss in 3ch sp, 3ch (counts as 1tr), 5tr in same sp, 1ch, (6tr, 1ch) in next 5 ch sps, ss in beg 3ch sp to finish.

Round 3: Change colour, *ss in 1ch sp, 3ch, [tr2tog] 3 times, 3ch, ss in 1ch sp, rep from * 5 times, ss in beg 1ch sp to finish.

Round 4: Change colour, *ss in 3ch sp, 4ch, tr3tog, 4ch, ss in next 3ch sp, 3ch, rep from * 5 times, ss in beg 3ch sp to finish.

Round 5: Change colour, 1dc in tr3tog from round 4, *4ch, 4dtr in next 3ch sp, 4ch, (1dc, 2ch, 1dc) in tr3tog, rep from * 5 times omitting last dc, ss in first dc to finish.

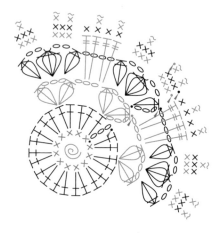

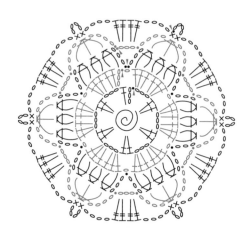

ROWAN

Materials

- 0.6mm (12 steel) crochet hook
- Gütermann hand quilting cotton in Turquoise 6934
- Embroidery needle

Finished size

20mm x 20mm (¾in x ¾in)

Round 1: Make a magic ring, 12dc in ring, ss in first dc.

Round 2: 5ch (counts as 1tr, 2ch), (1tr, 2ch) in every st, ss in third ch of beg 5ch.

Round 3: 1dc in beg tr, *5tr in next tr, (1dc, 3ch, 1dc) in next tr, rep from * 5 times omitting last 2ch and 1dc, 1htr in beg dc.

Round 4: 3ch (counts as 1tr), 1tr in same sp, *2ch, (1dc, 3ch, 1dc) in third tr of shell st, 2ch, 2tr in 3ch sp, 3ch picot st in tr just worked, 1tr in same sp, rep from * 5 times omitting last 2 tr and working the picot into the beg 3ch.

MOLLY

Materials

- 0.6mm (12 steel) crochet hook
- Gütermann hand quilting cotton in Red 1974
- Embroidery needle

Finished size

23mm x 23mm (⅞in x ⅞in)

Round 1: Make a magic ring, 7ch (counts as 1htr, 5ch) in ring, [1htr, 5ch] 5 times in ring, ss in second ch of beg 7ch.

Round 2: 4ch (counts as 1tr), (3tr, 4ch, ss) in 5ch sp (makes half a petal), *3ch, (ss, 4ch, 4tr) in next ch sp, 2ch, (4tr, 4ch ss) in next ch sp, rep from * once, 3ch, (ss, 4ch, 4tr) in next ch sp, 1ch, htr in beg 4ch.

Round 3: 4ch, 1tr in side of htr, *3ch, 1tr in 4ch sp on edge of petal, 3ch, dtr4tog in 3ch sp, 3ch, 1tr in 4ch sp, 3ch, (2tr, 2ch, 2tr) in 2ch sp, rep from * twice omitting last 2 tr, ss in beg 4ch to finish.

Round 4: *(ss, 2ch, 4tr, 2ch, ss) in next 4 3ch sps, ss between 2 tr sts, (2ch, 4tr, 2ch) in 2ch sp, ss between next 2 tr sts, rep from * twice with last ss being worked over ss from beg of round.

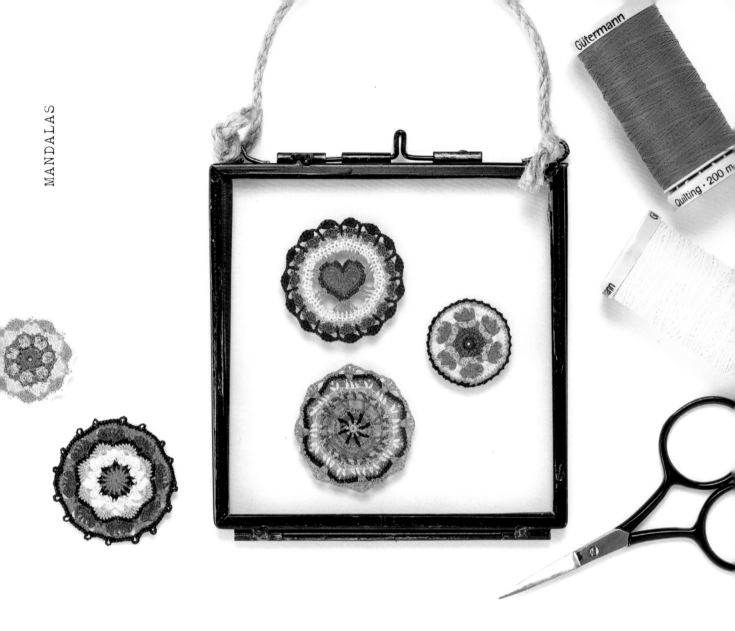

Framed mandala

Framing delicate crochet pieces is a lovely
way to decorate an office or craft room. This
project does not have to be made with just
mandalas, mix and match with any motif in this
book. Crochet pieces could even be teamed with
pressed flowers or family photographs for a
more sentimental composition.

Materials

- As many mandalas from this chapter as you wish to use in your frame
- Glass frame
- Brass sewing pins
- Tracing paper
- Masking tape or washi tape
- Cork board or foam core board (sometimes called sandwich board, available at most stationers) to pin your work to
- Double sided glass frame
- Window cleaner

Finished size

Same as frame size

The guides below can be traced for even pinning. If the mandala, for example, has 6 sides go for the hexagon shape, if it has 8 sides go for the octagon shape and so on.

When working on such small pieces differences in tension or mistakes can be quite easy to spot, so it is important to block a piece before framing to make it the perfect shape.

Trace your chosen diagram onto a piece of tracing paper. If your piece is bigger than the diagram, extend the lines going outwards to the desired length **(1)**.

Attach the tracing paper to the cork board or foam core board with tape. Make sure the side with the pencil marks is facing downwards so that the drawing cannot be transferred onto the crochet piece **(2)**.

Start by pinning the centre of the mandala to the centre of the diagram. You can pin sides, chain spaces or corner spaces depending on the nature of the crochet piece. Use corners or sides of the graph as a point of reference. You might be able to stretch your piece between the lines rather than on the lines, just make sure that all sides are the same. I find the best way to make sure that sides are equal is pinning opposite sides and corners **(3)** and **(4)**.

Leave to stretch for 24 hours, or lightly spray with water or fabric stiffener and leave to dry. Unpin and place inside the frame, making sure that both sides of the glass are thoroughly clean either by using a window spray, or vinegar and paper. Consider replacing the hanging of the frame with ribbon, string or crochet chain in matching colours.

If you are able to go into a shop to buy your glass frame, it is a good idea to test it in the shop with a crochet piece to check that the thickness of the crochet can be gripped between 2 sheets of glass. If you purchase a frame and find the gap between the two panes is too big, add a small dab of glue to the back of the centre and let it dry. You can also sew in an excess of thread to the centre, to add bulk so that the glass can grab onto it.

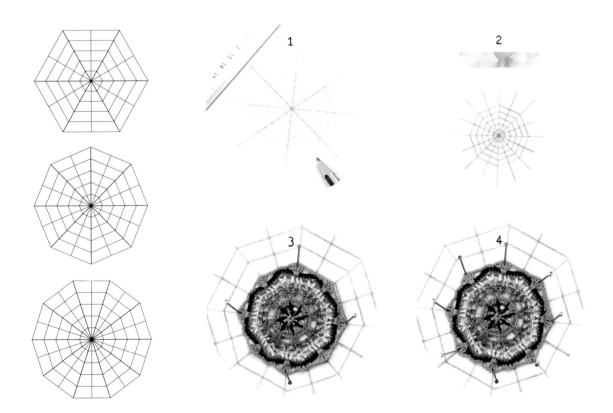

Bunting

The great thing about bunting is that it can be made with nearly all the motifs in this book. Mix and match motifs from different chapters to make unique pieces for cake toppers, jewellery, tiny bunting for your desk, or scale it up with DK wool for a statement piece that can be hung with pride in your living space. All use Gütermann top stitching thread with a 0.75mm (14/10 steel) hook. A 0.9mm (14/8 steel) or 1mm (12/6 steel) hook can also be used but will result in slightly bigger motifs.

TRIANGLE

Materials

- 0.75mm (14/10 steel) crochet hook
- Gütermann top stitching thread in Green 235
- Embroidery needle

Finished size

20mm x 23mm (¾in x ⅞in)

Round 1: Make a magic ring, 12dc in ring, ss in first dc.

Round 2: 8ch (counts as 1tr, 4ch), *skip 1 st, 1dc in next st, 4ch, skip 1 st, 1tr in next st, 4ch, rep from * once, skip 1 st, 1dc in next st, 4ch, ss in fourth ch of beg 8ch sp.

Round 3: *5dc in next two 4ch sps, 3ch, rep from * once more, 5dc in next two 4ch sps, 1ch, 1htr in beg dc to form last point.

Round 4: 1dc in 1htr sp, *(1ch, ss) in next 10 sts, (1dc, 3ch, 1dc) in 3ch sp, rep from * once more, (1ch, ss) in next 10 sts, 1dc in beg htr sp, 1ch, 1htr in beg dc.

STRIPED TRIANGLE

Materials

- 0.75mm (14/10 steel) crochet hook
- Gütermann top stitching thread, colours used in this order: Lilac 158, Green 235, Blue 714, Bright Pink 382, Light Green 152, Pink 758
- Embroidery needle

Finished size

20mm x 23mm (¾in x ⅞in)

Row 1: Make a magic ring, 1dc in ring (1 st).

Row 2: 1ch, turn, 2dc in next st (2 sts).

Row 3: 1ch, turn, 2dc in next 2 sts to finish (4 sts).

Row 4: Change colour, 2dc in first st of previous row, 1dc in each st to last st, 2dc in last st (6 sts).

Row 5: 1ch, turn work, 1dc in every st to finish.

Repeat rows 4 and 5 for each colour (12 sts).

CHEVRON

Materials

- 0.75mm (14/10 steel) crochet hook
- Gütermann top stitching thread, colours used in this order: Green 235, Light Green 152, Cream 414
- Embroidery needle

Finished size

17mm x 17mm (⅝in x ⅝in)

Row 1: Ch 13.

Row 2: 1dc in second ch from hook, 1dc in next 5 sts, 2ch, 1dc in next 6 sts.

Row 3: 1ch, turn, 1dc in first st, dc2tog, 1dc in next 3 sts, (1dc, 2ch, 1dc) in 2ch sp, 1dc in next 3 sts, dc2tog, 1dc in last st. ss to tighten last st and to finish.

Change colour, repeat row 3 twice.

Change colour, repeat row 3 twice.

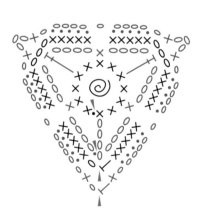

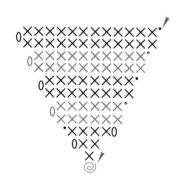

SPACE INVADER

Materials

- 0.75mm (14/10 steel) crochet hook
- Gütermann top stitching thread, colours used: Lilac 158 (yarn A), Purple 810 (yarn B), White 001
- Embroidery needle

Finished size

23mm x 21mm (⅞in x ¾in)

This is a great little exercise for trying out changing colours mid row. You need to carry 2 different threads as you crochet. I would recommend getting used to this technique with a chunky yarn first before going small.

Changing colour mid row

A colour change always begins one stitch before the actual colour change. On a row where the colour change is going to occur, crochet over the thread end of the second colour until one stitch before the colour change. In that stitch, crochet as normal, but swap colours on the very last 'yarn over pull through'. Use the new colour thread to continue, crocheting over the other thread as you go along.

Using yarn A make 15ch.

Rows 1 and 2: 1ch, turn, 1dc in next 15 sts.

Rows 3 to 10: Work as row 1, following the chart and changing colours where indicated.

Rows 11 and 12: Using yarn A only work as row 1.

Border

Using White and starting on last st of row 12, 1dc in next 14 sts, (1dc, 2ch, 1dc) in next st (makes corner), 1dc in next 12 row ends down side of bunting, (1dc, 2ch, 1dc) in next st/first starting ch, 1dc across next 14 ch, (1dc, 2ch, 1dc) in next ch/first row end, 1dc in next 11 sts, (1dc, 1ch, 1dc) in last corner st.

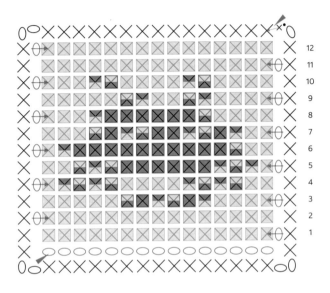

KEY

 Yarn A

 Yarn B

CHART NOTES

A box with a red surround means that the finished stitch should be the darker colour. The red arrows indicate the direction of the rows.

RAINBOW FLAG

Materials

- 0.75mm (14/10 steel) crochet hook
- Gütermann top stitching thread, colours used in this order: Red 156, Orange 982, Bright Orange 350, Green 235, Light Blue 714, Mid Blue 965, Purple 810
- Embroidery needle

Finished size

17mm x 13mm (⅝in x ½in)

Row 1: Ch 13.

Row 2: 1dc in second ch from hook, 1dc in next 11 sts to finish.

Row 3: Change colour, ss in beg st of prev row, 1dc in same st, 1dc in next 11 sts to finish.

Rows 4 to 8: Rep row 3 for each remaining colour.

LAYERED LEAF

Materials

- 0.75mm (14/10 steel) crochet hook
- Gütermann top stitching thread, colours used in this order: Light Green 152, Blue 714, Lilac 158
- Embroidery needle
- Soft toy stuffing

Finished size

19mm x 20mm (¾in x ¾in)

Round 1: Make a magic ring, 9dc in ring, ss in first dc to finish.

Round 2: Change colour, *(ss, 2ch, 2tr) in next st, 2ch, (2tr, 2ch, ss) in next st, 3ch, skip 1 st, rep from * twice, ss in same place as first ss to finish.

Round 3: Change colour, (ss, 3ch, 2dtr, 2ch, 2dtr, 3ch, ss) in one of the 3ch sps, 5ch, (ss, 3ch, 2dtr, 2ch, 2dtr, 3ch, ss) in the next 3ch sp, 5ch, (ss, 3ch, 2dtr, 1ttr, 4ch, ss in first ch (makes picot), 1ttr, 2dtr, 3ch, ss) in next 3ch sp, 5ch, ss in same place as first ss to finish.

HEART

Materials

- 0.75mm (14/10 steel) crochet hook
- Gütermann top stitching thread, colours used in this order: Light Pink 758, Green 235
- Embroidery needle

Finished size

17mm x 20mm (⅝in x ¾in)

Round 1: Make a magic ring. 4ch, [1tr, 2ch] twice into ring, [1dtr, 2ch] twice into ring, 1ttr, 3ch, 1ttr, [2ch, 1dtr] twice into ring, [2ch, 1tr] twice into ring, 4ch, ss in magic ring.

Round 2: Turn work, 1ch, 5dc in 4ch sp, 3dc in next ch sp, 2dc in next 3 ch sps, (2tr, 2ch, 2tr) in 3ch sp at bottom of heart, 2dc in next 3 ch sps, 3dc in next ch sp, 5dc in 4ch sp, 1ch, ss in magic ring to finish.

Round 3: Change colour, ss in magic ring, 1ch, 1dc in next 16 sts, (1dc, 3ch, 1dc) in 2ch sp at bottom of heart, 1dc in next 16 sts, 1ch, ss in magic ring to finish.

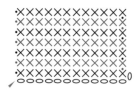

TEXTURED HEART

Materials

- 0.75mm (14/10 steel) crochet hook
- Gütermann top stitching thread, colours used: Lilac 158 (yarn A), Purple 810 (yarn B), White 001
- Embroidery needle

Finished size

16mm x 21mm (⅝in x ¾in)

This textured heart would look lovely with or without the colour change, either on bunting or part of a bigger piece like a blanket.

Using yarn A, ch 12.

Row 1: Turn work, 1dc in second ch from hook, 1dc in next 10 sts (11 sts).

Row 2: 1ch, turn, 1dc in next 11 sts.

Row 3: 1ch, turn, 1dc in next 5 sts changing to yarn B in last yarn over pull through of the last dc, 1FPtr in sixth st of row 1 changing to yarn A in last yarn over pull through, 1dc in next 5 sts.

Row 4: 1ch, turn, 1dc in next 11 sts, carrying yarn B along by working over it in the centre 3 sts of the row.

Row 5: 1ch, turn, 1dc in next 4 sts changing to yarn B in last yarn over pull through of the last dc, 1FPtr in fifth st of row 3, 1FPtr in next FPtr of row 3, 1FPtr in seventh st of row 3 changing to yarn A in last yarn over pull through, 1dc in rem 4 sts.

Row 6: 1ch, turn, 1dc in next 11 sts, carrying yarn B along by working over it in the centre 5 sts of the row.

Row 7: 1ch, turn, 1dc in next 3 sts changing to yarn B in last yarn over pull through of the last dc, 1FPtr in fourth st of row 5, 1FPtr in next 3 FPtr sts of row 5, 1FPtr in eighth st of row 5 changing to yarn A in last yarn over pull through, 1dc in rem 3 sts.

Row 8: 1ch, turn, 1dc in next 11 sts, carrying yarn B along by working over it in the centre 7 sts of the row.

Row 9: 1ch, turn, 1dc in next 2 sts changing to yarn B in last yarn over pull through of the last dc, 1FPtr in third st of row 7, 1FPtr in next 5 FPtr sts of row 7, 1FPtr in ninth st of row 7 changing to yarn A in last yarn over pull through, 1dc in rem 2 sts.

Row 10: As row 8.

Row 11: 1ch, turn, [1dc in next 3 sts changing to yarn B in last yarn over pull through of the last dc, FPtr3tog changing to yarn A in last yarn over pull through] twice, 1dc in last 3 sts.

Row 12: Cut yarn B, work as row 2 using yarn A.

Border

Using White and starting at the end of row 12, 1dc in each st and row end around 4 sides of the piece with (1dc, 2ch, 1dc) in the first 3 corner sts. On last corner, work 1dc, 1ch in corner st, 1dc into beg dc, ss to finish.

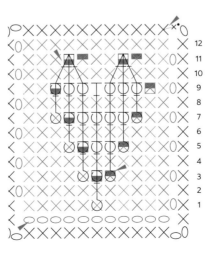

TINY BAG

Materials

- 0.75mm (14/10 steel) crochet hook
- Gütermann top stitching thread, colours used in this order: Lilac 158, Ecru 169
- Embroidery needle
- Small button

Finished size

17mm x 28mm (⅝in x 1⅛in)

This little pouch has numerous design possibilities depending on the yarn and hook size used. A tiny bag would make a beautiful stand-alone pendant, or crochet numerous ones a little bigger for a bunting-sized advent calendar. Don't forget to insert a tiny folded note when you have finished!

Row 1: Ch 11.

Row 2: 1dc in second ch from hook, 1dc in next 10 sts.

Row 3: 1ch, turn work, 1dc in next 10 sts.

Rows 4 to 33: Rep round 3. Add more repeats if you want the pouch to be longer.

Row 34 buttonhole: 1ch, turn work, 1dc in next 5 sts, 14ch, 1dc in eleventh ch from hook, 1dc in next 3 ch, 1dc in next 5 sts from row 33.

At this point, make sure that button or bead you will be using fits through the hole. If it is too small, increase the number of ch sts worked, before working the dc sts.

Row 35: 1ch, turn work, 1dc in next 4 sts, skip 1 st, 1dc in 4 sts up button loop, 12dc in buttonhole ch sp, 1dc in next 4 sts, skip 1 st, 1dc in remaining 4 sts, ss to finish.

Trim ends and weave in. Fold the sides, wrong sides facing inwards, as shown.

The bag can be joined by using crochet as described. Alternatively, the sides could be sewn together using a blanket or whip stitch.

Joining the Bag Sides

Using Ecru, make 1dc to join the 2 top left corners together, work 1dc through the row ends of each row down left side, joining the two edges together. Work 3dc in the bottom corner. Continue along the base, the next corner and the right side in the same way. Work 1dc in top right corner st, 2dc in same st on the front side only, continue along the front side only in the same way to the top left corner and work 2dc in the same place as the beg dc, ss in first dc, do not fasten off.

Buttonhole Edging

1ch, turn work, 1dc in next 4 sts, skip 1 st, 1dc in next 8 sts, 2 dc in next 2 sts, 1dc in next 8 sts, skip 1 st, 1dc in remaining 4 sts, ss in corner st on the front to join and finish. Trim and sew in ends. Sew a little button to the front of the piece.

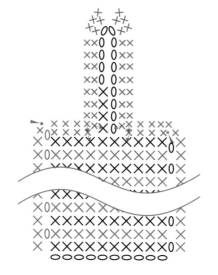

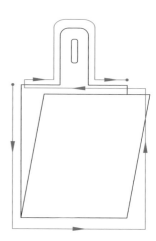

TINY HOUSE

Materials

- 0.75mm (14/10 steel) crochet hook
- Gütermann top stitching thread, colours used: **House**: Cream 169; **Roof**: Red 156; **Grass**: Light Green 152; **Door and window sash**: Brown 139; **Windows**: White 111; **Flower stalks**: Green 235; **Flowers**: Pink 758, Blue 714
- Embroidery needle
- Soft toy stuffing

Finished size

20mm x 25mm (¾in x 1in)

This house is adorable as a stand-alone crochet piece, a pendant, a plushie with thicker yarn, or as bunting to celebrate a new home. It is designed with two sides so it can be stuffed but it can also be made with one side as a flat motif. It features a little embroidery, so it can be customised with different flowers, windows or doors – you could even make one to look like your own house! It is worked from the top down.

House (make 2)

Row 1: Using Cream make a magic ring, 1dc in ring.

Row 2: Turn work, 1ch, 2dc in next st.

Row 3: Turn work, 1ch, 2dc in every st (4 sts).

Row 4: Turn work, 2dc in first st, 1dc in every st to the last st, 2dc in last st (6 sts).

Row 5: As row 3 (8 sts).

Row 6: As row 3 (10 sts).

Row 7: 1ch, do not turn work, work 1dc in each row end up side of roof triangle to row 1, (6 sts), 3ch, 1dc in each row end down other side of triangle back to row 6 (6 sts).

Row 8: 1ch, 1dc in every st (12 sts).

Rows 9 to 16: Turn work, 1ch, 1dc in every st to finish.

Row 17: Change to Green, 1dc in every st, work some of the sts randomly into rows 14 and 15 to make the row look like blades of grass.

Row 18: Turn work, 1ch, 1dc in every st to finish.

Roof

Using Red, ss in row 7 edge st, 1ch, 2dc in same st, 1dc in next 6 sts along roof slant, (3dc, 2ch, 3dc) in 3ch sp, 1dc in next 6 sts along other roof slant. (2dc, 1ch, ss) in edge st on other side of row 7.

Decorations

Using Cream embroider 2 little windows. Using Brown embroider a door to desired size and add texture with diagonal stitches for wooden slats. A French knot can be added for a doorknob and stitches can be added to outline the windows.

Work little running stitches along the side of the door and in the grass with the darker green.

Add little French knots for the flowers, pink ones for the rose trellis along the side of the door and blue ones in the grass for further decoration.

Other embroidery suggestions include adding a white picket fence, flowery window sills and birds.

Sewing and stuffing

Join the two halves together with the embroidery facing outwards. The roof and the grass areas can be sewn or crocheted together using the excess thread.

Either use whip stitch or work (ss, 1ch) in every st and (ss, 2ch, ss) in the roof point ch sp to keep it extra pointy.

Once the roof and grass areas are joined, whip stitch one of the cream house sides together. Stuff before sewing up the other side of the house.

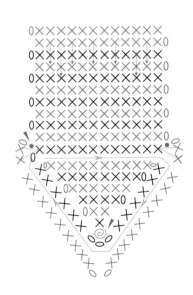

Cake topper

Bunting can brighten up an occasion, but tiny bunting creates an instant joy-factor at any party. Mix and match the colours and motifs from other chapters to make a cake topper that perfectly suits the celebration and the person you're celebrating.

Materials

- 0.75mm (14/10 steel) or 0.9mm (14/8 steel) crochet hook
- Gütermann top stitching thread in one of the colours used for your bunting
- Blocking materials such pins and foam core board
- BBQ skewers or something similar
- Decorative pieces like washi tape, small buttons, and thread scraps (optional)
- 2 small pegs or bulldog clips
- Adhesive such as PVA. Nail varnish will also do fine for this project.
- Scissors
- Sewing needle

Finished size

The height will be the same as the skewers

Crochet your elements and block

Make whichever bunting pieces you want to use. Decide on how many pieces there will be, how they will be arranged, and the desired distance between them. Bunting hangs best when there is an odd number like 5 or 7, so there is a central piece that hangs in the middle.

Block your pieces with pins and a foam core board. You can lightly spray them with water but it is not essential. Leave to set for a couple of hours (see Techniques: Blocking)

Connecting the pieces

Leave a long excess thread and make 20ch to start, ss behind each piece to connect, or work dc sts across the top of each bunting piece. When all pieces are connected make 20ch to finish, leaving a long excess thread (1).

(Optional) Decorate the BBQ skewers by wrapping decorative tape and thread scraps around them. Secure in place using glue and bulldog clips (2).

Use the excess thread from the bunting to secure it to the top of BBQ skewers. Add further decoration to the ends such as bows and buttons (3).

1

2

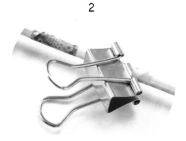

3

Animals

This chapter contains a cute mix of layered motifs and animal faces that would be ideal for jewellery or children's items. You could even customise some of the features and colours of the dog or cat to make them look like your own pets!

The animals are worked using Gütermann hand quilting cotton with a 0.5mm-0.6mm (12 steel) hook or Gütermann top stitching thread with a 0.75mm (14/10 steel) hook. A 0.9mm (14/8 steel) hook will work just as well but may produce slightly larger pieces.

BUMBLEBEE

Materials

- 0.6mm (12 steel) or 0.75mm (14/10 steel) crochet hook
- Gütermann hand quilting cotton (if using 0.6mm/12 steel hook), colours used: Yellow 758, Black 5201, White 5709. Choose similar colours in Gütermann top stitching thread if using 0.75mm (14/10 steel) hook
- Embroidery needle
- Small amount of stuffing (scrap yarn recommended)

Finished size

15mm x 15mm x 15mm (⅝in x ⅝in x ⅝in)

Round 1: Using Yellow make a magic ring, into ring work 8dc, ss in beg dc (8 sts).

Round 2: 2dc in every st, ss in beg dc (16 sts).

Round 3: [2dc in next st, 1dc in next st] to end, ss in beg dc (24 sts).

Round 4: 1dc in every st, ss in beg dc.

Rounds 5 to 6: Change to Black, 1dc in every st, ss in beg dc.

Rounds 7 to 8: Change to Yellow, 1dc in every st, ss in beg dc.

Rounds 9 to 10: Change to Black, 1dc in every st, ss in beg dc.

Embroider the face using Black and start stuffing the bee.

Round 11: Change to Yellow, 1dc in every st, ss in beg dc.

Round 12: [dc2tog, 1dc] to end (16 sts).

Round 13: 1dc, [dc2tog, 1dc] to end (11 sts).

Round 14: 1dc, [dc2tog] to end (6 sts).

Add more stuffing or scrap yarn. Sew the remaining hole closed and trim the ends.

Bee Wings (make 2)

Row 1: Using White make a magic ring, into ring work 3ch, [1dtr, 1ch] twice, 1dtr, 3ch, ss.

Row 2: 1ch, turn work, 4dc in 3ch sp, 3dc in next two 1ch sps, 4dc in beg 3ch sp, 1ch, ss in magic ring.

Use thread ends to sew the wings to the body.

MOUSE

Materials

- 0.6mm (12 steel) crochet hook
- Gütermann hand quilting cotton, colours used: Grey 6506, Pink 3526, Dark Navy 5322
- Embroidery needle
- Small amount of stuffing (scrap yarn recommended)
- Nail Varnish

Finished size

13mm x 13mm x 10mm (½in x ½in x ⅜in)

Round 1: Using Grey make a magic ring, into ring work 8dc (8 sts).

Round 2: Work in a spiral, 2dc in every st (16 sts).

Round 3: 1dc, [2dc in next st, 1dc in next st] to end (21 sts).

Rounds 4 to 6: 1dc in every st.

Round 7: 1dc in every st.

Round 8: 1dc, [3dc, dc2tog] to end (17 sts).

Start stuffing at this point.

Round 9: 2dc, [3dc, dc2tog] to end (14 sts).

Round 10: 2dc, [dc2tog, 2dc] to end (11 sts).

Round 11: 1dc, [dc2tog] to end (6 sts).

Add more stuffing or scrap yarn. Change to Pink and embroider the hole closed to create a nose, trim the ends.

Ears (make 2)

Row 1: Using Pink make a magic ring, into ring work 3ch, 3tr, 3ch, ss.

Row 2: Change to Grey, ss in magic ring, 2ch, 2dc in 3ch sp, 2dc in next 2 sp between sts, 2dc in last ch sp, 2ch, ss in magic ring.

Tail

Using Grey work 10ch, dab nail varnish onto end before trimming to stop from fraying.

Use thread ends to sew the ears and tail to the body as shown in the photograph.

Embroider the eyes as shown in the photograph using Dark Navy.

BIRD

Materials

- 0.6mm (12 steel) crochet hook
- Gütermann hand quilting cotton, colours used in this order: Faun Brown 1225, Dark Red 2833, Dusky Teal 7325, Dark Red 2833 (again), Faun Brown 1225 (again); **Eyes**: Dark Navy 5322; **Beak**: Yellow 758
- Embroidery needle
- Small amount of stuffing (scrap yarn recommended)

Finished size

13mm x 13mm x 10mm (½in x ½in x ⅜in)

Round 1: Using Faun Brown make a magic ring, into ring work 8dc (8 sts).

Round 2: Work in a spiral, 2dc in every st (16 sts).

Round 3: 1dc, [2dc in next st, 1dc in next st] to end (21 sts).

Rounds 4 to 6: 1dc in every st.

Round 7: Change to Dark Red, 1dc in every st.

Round 8: 1dc, [3dc, dc2tog] to end (17 sts).

Start stuffing at this point.

Round 9: Change to Dusky Teal, 2dc, [3dc, dc2tog] to end (14 sts).

Round 10: 2dc, [dc2tog, 2dc] to end (11 sts).

Round 11: 1dc, [dc2tog] to end (6 sts).

Add more stuffing or scrap yarn. Sew the remaining hole closed and trim the ends.

Wings (make 2)

Row 1: Using Dark Red make a magic ring, into ring work 4ch, 4dtr, 4ch, ss.

Row 2: Change to Faun Brown, ss in top of first dtr from row 1, dtr4tog in sp between each st.

Use thread ends to sew the wings to the body as shown in the photograph.

Embroider the eyes as shown in the photograph using Dark Navy.

Beak

Using Yellow, ss in the bird head between the eyes on row 2 or 3, 1ch, 2htr, 2ch, ss in same st.

Use thread ends to further secure and position the beak on the head.

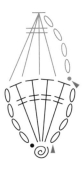

BUNNY

Materials

- 0.6mm (12 steel) crochet hook
- Gütermann hand quilting cotton, colours used: Bright Pink 2955, Mustard Yellow 956
- Embroidery needle

Finished size

20mm x 12mm (¾in x ½in)

Round 1: Using Bright Pink make a magic ring, into ring work 2ch, 10htr, ss in beg 2ch.

The beginning and end of rounds marks the base of the rabbit where the tail will go.

Round 2: 2ch, 3htr in next 2 sts, 1htr in next 2 sts, 2htr in next 2 sts, 1htr in next 2 sts, 3htr in last 2 sts, ss in 2ch.

Round 3: 1ch, 2dc in next 6 sts, 1dc in next 3 sts, (ss, 4ch, 2dtr) in next st* (for head), (4ch, 1dtr, 4ch, ss) in dtr st just made (for ear), 1dtr in same htr as at*, mirror the sts already worked for the other half of the bunny, ss in beg ch.

Round 4: 1ch, 1dc in next 15 sts, 4dc in 4ch sp for head, 1dc in first dtr, ss in second dtr at base of ear, 4dc in 4ch sp for ear, (1dc, 2ch, 1dc) in dtr st, 4dc in second ch sp for ear, ss in dtr at base of ear, 1dc in next dtr, mirror sts already worked for the other half of the bunny, ss in beg ch.

Tail

Using Mustard Yellow make a magic ring and work [1dc, 3ch] ten times into the ring, ss in ring.

Use threads ends to sew the tail onto the bunny body.

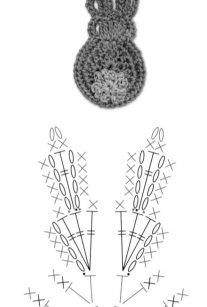

FOX FACE

Materials

- 0.75mm (14/10 steel) or 0.90mm (14/8 steel) crochet hook
- Gütermann top stitching thread, colours used: Fox Orange 982, White 800, Dark Red 369; **For embroidery**: Dark Red 369, Green 235, White 800
- Embroidery needle

Finished size

22mm x 20mm (⅞in x ¾in)

Row 1: Using Fox Orange make a magic ring, into ring work 1ch, 1dc. Do not pull the magic ring too tightly.

Row 2: 1ch, turn, 1dc.

Row 3: 1ch, turn, 2dc in next st.

Row 4: 1ch, turn, 1dc in next 2 sts.

Row 5: 1ch, turn, 2dc in the next 2 sts.

Row 6: 1ch, turn, 2dc in the next st, 1dc in next 2 sts, 2dc in last st.

Row 7: 1ch, turn, 2dc in first st, 1dc in next 4 sts, 2dc in last st.

Row 8: 1ch, turn, 2dc in first st, 1dc in next 6 sts, 2dc in last st.

Row 9: 3ch, turn, (1tr, 1dtr, 3ch picot) in first st, (1tr, 3ch, ss) in next st. 1dc in next 2 sts, 1htr in next 2 sts, 1dc in next 2 sts, (ss, 3ch, 1tr) in next st, (1dtr, 3ch picot, 1tr, 3ch, ss) in last st.

Row 10: Starting in same st, 8dc down side of face, 1dc in magic ring (9 sts all together), 3ch, 1dc in magic ring, 8dc up other side of face (9 sts all together) ss in last st of row 8.

Cheeks

Using White and working in back loops only, ss in second dc from nose, ss in next st, 1htr in next st, 2dtr in next 2 sts, 1htr in next st, ss in next 2 sts, ending in last st of row 10. Repeat on left side of face, starting in first st of row 10 and ending in eighth st.

Nose

Using Dark Red (ss, 1ch, 1dc, 1ch, ss) in 3ch sp from row 10.

Embroider the eyes using Dark Red and Green. Embroider the ears using White.

BUTTERFLY

Materials

- 0.6mm (12 steel) crochet hook
- Gütermann hand quilting cotton, colours used in this order: Orange 2045, Bright Red 2074, Black 5201, Dark Red 2833
- Embroidery needle

Finished size

18mm x 18mm (¾in x ¾in)

Wings

Round 1: Make a magic ring, into ring work 6ch, 2htr, 3ch, 2tr, 3ch, 2htr, 3ch, 1tr, ss in third ch of beg 6ch.

Round 2: (5ch, 2ttr, 3dtr, 4ch, ss) in 3ch sp, ss between htr sts, (ss, 4ch, 3tr, 4ch, ss) in next 3ch sp, ss between tr sts, (ss, 4ch, 3tr, 4ch, ss) in next 3ch sp, ss between htr sts, ss in last 3ch sp, (4ch, 3dtr, 2ttr, 5ch, ss) in last 3ch sp.

Round 3: Change colour, ss in beg 3ch sp from round 1, 1ch, (4dc, 1htr) in 5ch sp, (2tr, 2ch, 1tr) in first ttr, 1tr in next 4 sts, 5tr in 4ch sp, 3ch, ss in same 3ch sp from round 1, ss between htr sts from round 1, ss in next 3ch sp from round 1, 2ch, 3htr in 4ch sp, 1htr in next 3 sts, 3htr in 4ch sp, 2ch, ss in same 3ch sp from round 1, ss between tr sts from round 1, mirror sts worked so far for rest of round.

Round 4: Change colour, ss in beg 3ch sp from round 1, 1ch, 1dc in next 7 sts (1dc, 2ch, 1dc) in 2ch sp, 1dc in next 10 sts, 3dc in 3ch sp, ss in same 3ch sp from round 1, ss between htr sts from round 1, ss in next 3ch sp from round 1, 1ch, 2dc in 2ch sp, 1dc in next 9 sts, 2dc in 2ch sp, 1ch, ss in same 3ch sp from round 1, ss between tr sts from round 1, mirror sts worked so far for rest of round.

Body

Using Dark Red, ss between 2 tr sts of round 1, (6ch, ttr4tog, ss) in same place. Sew the top of the body to the top of the butterfly between the two bigger wings. This should cover round 1 and connecting ss sts.

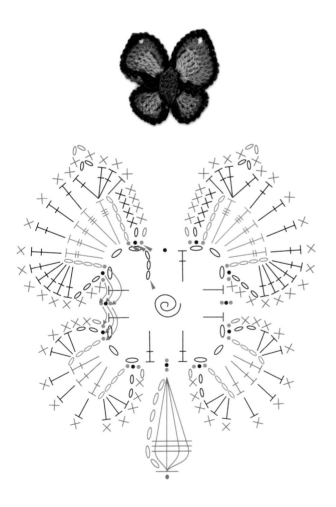

CAT FACE

Materials

- 0.6mm (12 steel) crochet hook
- Gütermann hand quilting cotton, colours used: Light Grey 618, Pink 3526, Black 5201, Grey 6506; **For embroidery:** Black 5201
- Embroidery needle

Finished size

15mm x 15mm (⅝in x ⅝in)

Round 1: Using Light Grey make a magic ring, into ring work 8dc, ss in beg dc.

Round 2: 1dc in beg st, 3tr in next 2 sts, 1dc in next 2 sts, 3tr in next 2 sts, 1dc in next st, ss in beg dc.

Round 3: 2dc in every st, ss in beg dc (32 sts).

Round 4: 1dc in every st, ss in beg dc, but do not trim end.

Ears

Join Pink in the fourth st to the left from beg of round 4, (ss, 2ch, 2tr, 2ch, 2tr, 2ch, ss) in same st as beg ss.

Join Pink in the fourth st to the right from beg of round 4, (ss, 2ch, 2tr, 2ch, 2tr, 2ch, ss) in same st as beg ss.

Outer edge

Round 5: Pick up Light Grey from round 4, 1dc in next 3 sts, ss in next st at base of ear, 2ch, 2dc in 2ch sp, 1dc between 2 tr sts (1dc, 2ch, 1dc) in 2ch sp, 1dc between 2 tr sts, 2tr in 2ch sp, 1dc in next st on edge of cat face, 1dc in each st until second ear is reached, 2dc in 2ch sp, 1dc between 2 tr sts, (1dc, 2ch, 1dc) in 2ch sp, 1dc between 2 tr sts, 2dc in 2ch sp, 2ch, ss in st at base of ear, 1dc in 3 remaining sts, ss in beg dc. Fasten off.

Nose and Muzzle

Using Light Grey make a magic ring, into ring work 2ch, 4tr (changing to Black in last st), 3tr to make nose (changing to Grey in last st), 4tr, 2ch, ss.

Use threads ends to sew Nose and Muzzle onto cat face. Use Black to embroider the eyes, marks on the cheeks and forehead and a partition between the cheeks and mouth if desired.

DOG FACE

Materials

- 0.6mm (12 steel) crochet hook
- Gütermann hand quilting cotton, colours used: Light Ivory 919, Fawn Brown 1225, Brown 1833, Pink 3526; **For embroidery:** Black 5201
- Embroidery needle

Finished size

18mm x 15mm (¾in x ⅝in)

Face with Patch

Round 1: Using Light Ivory make a magic ring, into ring work 8dc, ss to beg dc.

Round 2: 3ch, 4tr in first dc, 1dc in next 2 sts (changing to Fawn Brown in last st), 4tr in next st (changing to Light Ivory in last st), 4tr in next st, 1dc in next 2 sts, 4tr in last st, ss in beg 3ch.

Round 3: 3ch, 2tr in next 4 sts, 1dc in next 2 sts (changing to Fawn Brown in last st), 2htr In next 4 sts (changing to Light Ivory in last st), 2htr in next 4 sts, 1dc in next 2 sts, 2tr in next 4 sts, ss in beg 3ch.

Nose and Muzzle

Using Light Ivory make a magic ring, into ring work 4ch, 5dtr (changing to Brown in last st), 4dtr (changing to Ivory in last st), 5dtr, 4ch, ss in magic ring, close magic ring but not too tightly.

Change to Pink for tongue, (ss, 3ch, 1tr, 3ch, ss) in magic ring between the 2 ch sps.

Ears (make 2)

Row 1: Using Fawn Brown make a magic ring, into ring work 5ch (counts as dtr), 4ttr.

Row 2: Turn work, 5tr in third ttr to make shell stitch, ss in fifth ch of beg 5ch sp.

Use thread end to sew the pieces together. Use black thread to embroider eyes just above the muzzle.

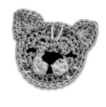

HEN

Materials

- 0.6mm (12 steel) crochet hook
- Gütermann hand quilting cotton, colours used: Brown 1833, Black 5201, Red 2453, Mustard Yellow 956
- Embroidery needle

Finished size

14mm x 12mm (½in x ½in)

Round 1: Using Brown make a magic ring, into ring work 10dc, ss in first dc.

Round 2: 3ch, 2tr in the next 8 sts.

Round 3: 3ch, turn work, 4tr in same st, [[ss in next st, 3tr in next st] twice, dc in the next 9 sts, skip 1 st, 7tr in last tr, ss around 3ch sp.

Wing (make 2)

Using Brown make a magic ring, into ring work 3ch, 1tr, (3ch, ss) in same st (makes picot), 1dtr, 3ch picot, 1ttr, 3ch picot, 5ch, ss in magic ring.

Head

Using Red ss in fifth st of 7tr shell of the head, (1ch, 1dc, 2ch, 1dc) in same st, 2ch, (1dc, 2ch, 1dc, 1ch, ss) in next st to finish.

Chin

Using Red work (ss, 1ch, 1dc, 1ch, ss) in last dc of round 3.

Beak

Using Mustard Yellow (ss, 3ch, ss) in third st of 7tr shell of the head.

ELEPHANT

Materials

- 0.6mm (12 steel) crochet hook
- Gütermann hand quilting cotton, colours used: **Body and ears**: Grey 6506; **Eyes**: Dark Navy 5322
- Embroidery needle
- Glue or nail varnish

Finished size

20mm x 10mm (¾in x ⅜in)

Round 1: Using Grey make a magic ring, into ring work 2ch, 10htr, ss in beg htr. The end of round is the tail-end of the elephant.

Round 2: 2ch, 3htr in first st, 2htr in next 3 sts, 3htr in next 2 sts, 2htr in next 3 sts, 3htr in last st, ss in beg htr.

Round 3: 1ch, 1dc in next 4 sts, (2ch, 1tr, 2ch, ss) in same st as the last dc was worked to make back leg, 1dc in next 4 sts, (ss, 2ch, 1tr, 2ch, 1dc) in next st to make second leg, 1dc in next 3 sts, 8ch, 1dc in second ch from hook, skip 1 ch, 1dc in next ch, skip 1 ch, 1dc in next 3 ch, 1dc in same st at base of trunk to make tail, 1dc in next 12 sts, ss in beg ch, 4ch, ss in last ch to make tail end.

Add a tiny bit of glue or nail varnish to the end of the tail to make sure it is secure before cutting the yarn end.

Ears (make 2)

Round 1: Using Grey make a magic ring, into ring work 3ch, 2tr, 2dtr, 4ch, ss.

Round 2: 3ch, turn work, 4htr in 4ch sp, 1dc between each following pair of sts 4 times, 3ch, ss in magic ring.

Use thread ends to sew ears to the elephant body.

Use Dark Navy thread to embroider the eyes.

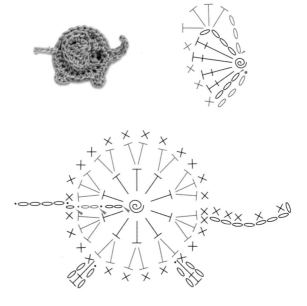

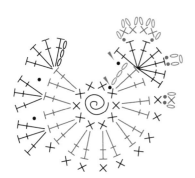

Meadow embroidery hoop

This project nicely brings together a mix of materials and motifs from other chapters. It also introduces a little wire work that you would typically use in jewellery making to add rigidity and structure to the leaves. This project incorporates pieces from the animal, floral and leaf chapters but you can mix and match motifs in any way you wish!

I chose a brass coloured wire because it coordinated with the screw fastening of the hoop, but you can get wire in lots of different colours. Jewellery wire that has a bright colour is usually referred to as enamel coated wire and it has a copper, brass or nickel core.

Materials

- 0.6mm (12 steel) crochet hook if using hand quilting cotton or 0.8mm (13 steel) crochet hook if you are using top stitching thread
- Gütermann hand quilting cotton for the butterflies, bees, flowers and leaves in whatever colour you want. I used the ones mentioned in the individual patterns.
- Small embroidery hoop, I used a 10cm (4in) hoop
- Masking tape and/or E600 glue
- Jewellery wire, 26 gauge/0.45mm in diameter or thicker.
- Flat nose pliers
- Cutting pliers
- Round nose pliers, or alternatively, something that you can wrap wire around like a thin crochet hook
- Beads for flower centres
- Scissors
- Sewing needle
- Beads, buttons, dried flowers, charms (optional for extra decoration)

Finished size

Same as embroidery hoop used

Map out your composition

Making a quick and simple sketch of your hoop will help you plan the size, shape, composition of your elements and wire lengths needed. It also saves you from making too many. I drew around my hoop for size, and sketched my pieces knowing that I can change it up as I progress through the project **(1)**.

Crochet your elements and add the wire

To attach wire to the back of the butterfly cut a length of wire that is longer than you need. Using cotton that is the same colour as the butterfly body, sew a few stitches to trap the wire. Make a sharp fold of the wire and continue to sew, trapping the wire as you go **(2)**.

To attach wire to the back of the bee prise a hole through the stitches and stuffing at the back of the bee with a fine crochet hook. Thread the wire through, make a sharp fold with pliers, thread that end through another stitch and pull back through. You should only see a slight bend in the wire at the top of the bee. Trim any excess wire with pliers **(3)**.

Make the small round leaves using the pattern for the Bee Wings with Mid Green 8724. Thread a long length of wire through the magic ring and wrap the wire to secure. Trim the excess wire or curl it with pliers for extra decoration **(4)**.

On the bigger leaves, you can 'crochet in' wire around the edge of a leaf as you would excess thread from a previous round. Start by crocheting a few stitches, trapping the wire, then bending the tip of the wire with pliers so it cannot come undone. Crochet in the rest of the wire, trapping the bent tip as you go along **(5)**.

Bend the end of the wire at a right angle for attaching elements, then tape them to the inner hoop from the front and the back for extra dimension. You could also wrap the wire around the hoop, but this makes it more difficult to rearrange the pieces **(6)**.

Once all the pieces are rearranged, add the outer hoop to trap the pieces and hide the tape. Use pliers on the screw to tighten the hoop further. E600 glue can be added to the back if there are any wobbly pieces that need reinforcement.

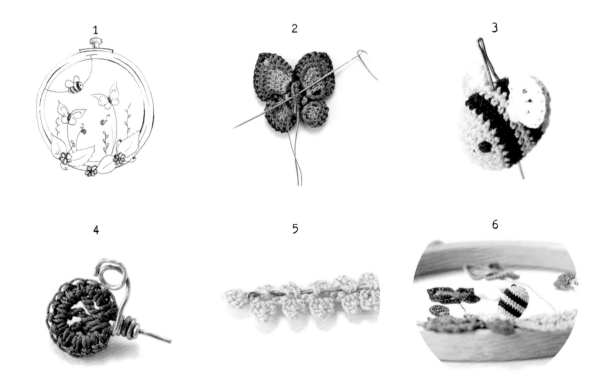

1

2

3

4

5

6

Techniques

In this section, you will learn about useful stitches, stuffing, blocking and starching, and my specialty, which is turning your micro-crochet into incredibly special jewellery pieces.

Crocheting small

Holding your work

There are lots of different ways in which the thread and hook can be held for a comfortable crochet experience with even tension. Most of the time it is easier to hold them in the same way as you would when crocheting something bigger, but here are some things that I do that may be useful for crocheting small:

I find the pencil position most comfortable for micro-crochet rather than the knife position **(1)**. This way you can rest your middle finger on top of the loops already on the hook to stop them sliding off or becoming loose, without losing visibility of what you are making.

I wrap the thread around my index finger as shown to give an even tension **(2)**.

I hold a crocheted piece in my non-hook hand with the tip of my thumb and the side of my middle finger for better visibility **(3)**.

I also sometimes use a rubber or plastic thimble for the non-hook hand middle finger. This is particularly good for protecting fingers when using minute hooks and starting a crochet piece that is done in rows, especially when crocheting onto a foundation row of tiny chain stitches. Alternatively, you can wrap your finger in washi tape, masking tape or a plaster.

Starting out

For beginners, look for patterns where you crochet into stitch or chain spaces rather than actual stitches, especially if you have particularly tight tension. An example of this is Denise in the Mandala chapter.

Start with a big hook, like a 3mm (1 steel), a thicker yarn, and gradually work your way down the hook and thread sizes. If you can't go any smaller than 2mm (4 steel), don't worry, you'll still make delightfully small crochet pieces. The joy of making is more important than crocheting small.

Experiment with different hook sizes for the thread you are using. There is more information on thread thicknesses in the Tools and Materials section.

Choose lighter coloured threads instead of dark ones, as dark threads and stitches can be hard to see..

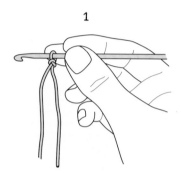

1

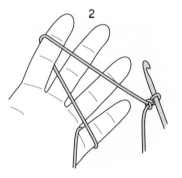

2

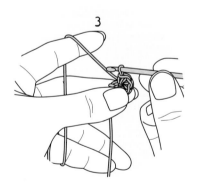

3

Yarning over

There are different areas to micro crochet that you can subtly adapt to create your own special technique. You can play around with tension, the way you hold your hook and thread, hook and thread gauges, and also the way that you yarn over.

Yarning over so that the loops are positioned close together and closer to the hook helps to make smaller and tighter stitches. Position the middle finger of your hook hand on the loops to stabilise them as you practise micro crochet **(4)**.

Yarning over so that the loops are further apart will make longer looser stitches. Again, position the middle finger of your hook hand on the loops to stabilise them, as working this way means that there is no chance of varying the tension by accident **(5)**.

Saving time

Crochet in loose ends when you change colours and begin a new row or round on a motif so that there are fewer threads to sew in afterwards. Not only does this save time but it is often neater and more secure, just pull the excess thread taut before trimming off.

Taking care

A hands-free magnifier will also be very useful for beginners, even if you have good eyesight.

Crocheting in natural light is a given regardless of the size of your crochet projects. However, if you are crocheting outside on a sunny day, try and crochet in the shade. Most small hooks are steel and shiny, and the flash of reflection from the sun as the hook moves is distracting and bad for your eyes.

Sewing in ends

John James bead embroidery needles in size 10 are great for sewing in those pesky ends when crocheting with finer threads. They are very strong considering their fineness, and the eye of the needle is slim so the crochet stitches don't stretch as you pass it through.

4

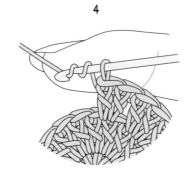

5

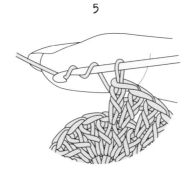

Crochet basics

Crochet stitch terminology

Each motif in this book has a diagram and a crochet pattern written in UK crochet terms. This chart shows what each stitch abbreviation or symbol means alongside the US equivalent where relevant.

Abbreviation	Symbol	UK meaning	US meaning (if different)
ss	●	Slip stitch	
ch	⬯	Chain stitch	
dc	✕	Double crochet	**sc** Single crochet
dc2tog	⋏✕	2 double crochet together, used for reducing the amount of stitches on a row or a round	**sc2tog** 2 single crochet together, used for reducing the amount of stitches on a row or a round
htr	T	Half treble crochet	**hdc** Half double crochet
tr	⊤	Treble crochet	**dc** Double crochet
dtr	⊤	Double treble crochet	**tr** Treble crochet
ttr	⊤	Triple treble crochet	**dtr** Double treble crochet
trtog eg. tr4tog	⬯	Treble stitches together, eg. 4 treble stitches together	**dctog** Double stitches together, eg. 4 double stitches together
back-dc	⨯̃	Back double crochet or crab stitch	**back-sc** Back single crochet or crab stitch
FP eg. 2FPtr	⌒⊺	Front post crochet, eg. 2 front post treble crochet stitches	Front post crochet, eg. 2 front post double crochet stitches
BP eg. 2BPtr	⌒⊺	Back post crochet, eg. 2 back post treble crochet stitches	Back post crochet, eg. 2 back post double crochet stitches
PC	⬯	Popcorn stitch	
	⌒	Crochet into back loop only	
	⌣	Crochet into front loop only	

Reading a crochet chart

Some crocheters like written patterns, some prefer diagrams, and others rely on both. As a visual learner I am a diagram reader as I find it easier to track my progress and understand the reasoning for certain stitches in future rounds.

WORKING IN ROWS

Referring to the pattern to see how many foundation chains are needed, start at **(1)**. Follow the pattern from right to left on the first row **(2)**. Follow the pattern from left to right on the second row **(3)**. Slip stitch to finish, start next colour with a slip stitch **(4)**. Look out for overlayed thin arrows as they can indicate a different stitch pattern **(5)**.

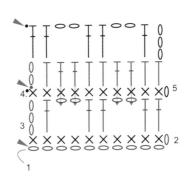

WORKING IN ROUNDS

Crochet diagrams worked in the round start at the centre. Look for the spiral which indicates a magic ring.

Most rounds start with chain stitches and finish with a slip stitch.

Special stitches

Magic circle or ring

The magic circle can be tricky, but once mastered, will be your best friend in micro-crochet. It allows you to quickly start working on a flat shape in the round and it allows you to leave the hole closed or open for sewing a bead in the centre. It is particularly good for crocheting flowers.

Wrap the thread around two of your fingers twice **(1)**.

Place the hook under the two threads, yarn over hook and pull through **(2)**.

Crochet the first round of your pattern, keeping your fingers in the ring for support for as long as needed **(3)**.

Remove hook and fingers to reveal the two loops on the magic ring and the excess thread. Tug that excess thread, one of the loops should begin to shrink **(4)**. Pick that loop and pull to draw the other one to a complete close **(5)**.

Pull the excess thread again to pull the last loop to a close. You can then slip stitch the first stitch or continue to work in a spiral.

Magic ring alternative

An alternative to the magic ring is crocheting a chain of 6 to 8 stitches, slip stitch to join, crochet your first round, sew around the back of the stitches using the thread end and drawing to a close like a drawstring bag.

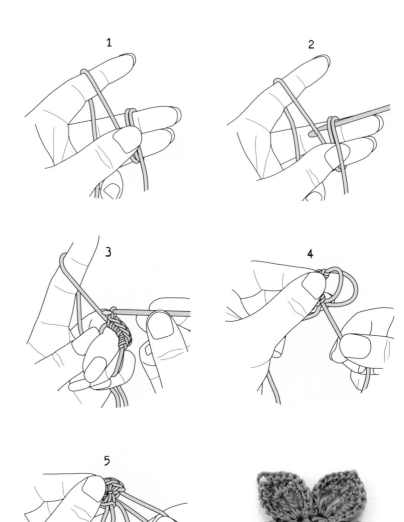

Back-double crochet or crab stitch

This is a pretty edging stitch that can add structure or flatten out pieces that may have cupped a little while crocheting. You can easily skip stitches, and chain stitches in between them, or layer it up by crocheting over a pre-existing back-double crochet row to give bulk and extra decoration. You can see a good example of this on the Mattea mandala pattern.

Start the round with a slip stitch, or the slip stitch from the previous round. Place hook in the stitch to the right instead of the left (**6**), yarn over pull through stitch (**7**), yarn over pull through both loops as you would a double crochet stitch (**8**).

Crochet your last back-double crochet in the position where the beginning slip stitch was made. Make a finishing slip stitch in the top of the first back-double crochet to make the join seamless (**9**).

Back-double crochet is not great for edging sharp corners, so here's a tip. Turn your work just before the corner so that you are working forwards instead of backwards, work (1dc, 2ch, 1dc) in a chain space or stitch where you want the corner to be, turn your work again and continue to crochet the back-double crochet backwards along the edge.

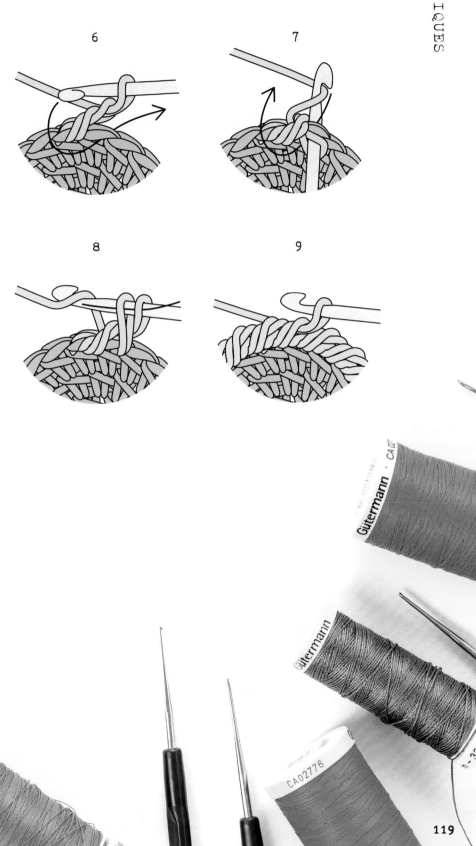

Ss, 1ch edging

A simple (ss, 1ch) in each stitch is an edging that gives a beautiful plaited affect. This is a simple alternative to back-double crochet (crab stitch) and doesn't require you to work backwards.

Surface crochet

This can be worked on flat motifs or 3D pieces and makes a nice alternative to embroidery. It is a slip stitch across the surface rather than the edge **(1)**. You can 'hook' the yarn from either below the crochet piece or from above, which is easier when working on 3D pieces that have already been stuffed.

Whip stitch

Crocheted pieces can be joined together using whip stitch, either through the back loops **(2)** or through both loops at the top of your crochet stitches.

Invisible slip stitch

Sometimes finishing a round with a standard slip stitch on a beginning chain stitch can make it obvious where the round starts and ends. This 'invisible' method can take a little more time, but it makes the round seamless, which can be important on a finishing edging or on a round of shell stitches.

Pull out the thread on the last stitch of a row without making a slip stitch first.

Use a hook or needle to thread the end though the two top loops of the beginning stitch, where you would normally crochet a stitch **(3)**.

Thread the end though the top of the last stitch and sew in place at the back. Make sure not to do this too tightly or the stitch could pucker.

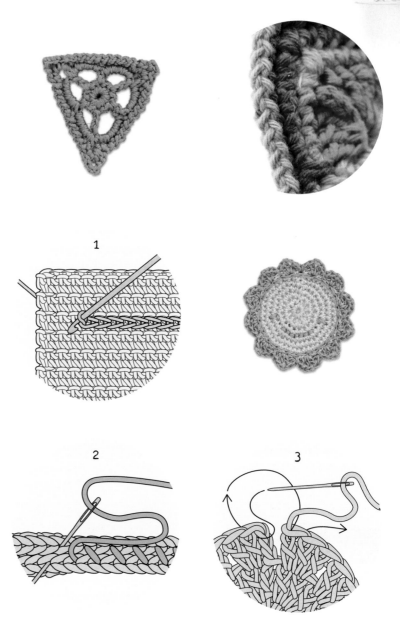

1

2

3

Changing colour half-way through a row

The principle for changing colour half-way through a row is the same as in standard-sized crochet. Whether it be a double, treble or double-treble crochet stitch, it begins at the stitch before the colour change.

The chart below shows where the colour change happens by showing a stitch with the bottom half in the old colour and the top half in the new colour.

Make a stitch as you usually would, stopping before the last 'yarn over, pull through'. Swap colours on the last 'yarn over pull through' to complete the colour change and use that colour for the next stitch or stitches **(4)**.

Remember to crochet-in the other thread which is not in use, ready to change back again when needed **(5)**.

4

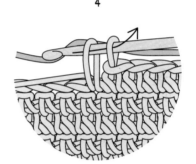

5

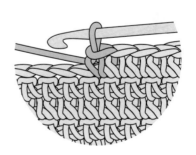

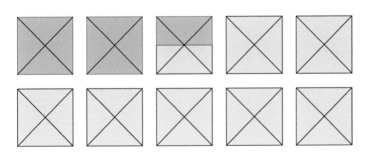

Stiffening

I only use fabric stiffener when a crochet piece is very lacy, such as holly leaves and snowflakes. Pieces that need to be shaped can also be pinned in place, lightly sprayed with water and left to air dry.

For a crochet piece that is geometric in appearance and requires even blocking, draw guidance lines on a small piece of tracing paper. See below for ready-made guidance lines that can be traced. Stick the tracing paper drawn-side down on some foam core board or a surface that can hold pins.

Mix half and half liquid fabric stiffener and room temperature water in a small bowl. You can experiment with the ratios, the more stiffener in the mix, the more ridged the piece will become.

Soak the crochet piece in the solution for 5 minutes or so. They may shrink further but they can be stretched when pinning. At this point you need to make sure that your hands, nails, pin board and tea towels are free from fibres, dirt and debris as they can stick to the crochet piece.

Remove the piece from the solution and dab off any excess liquid with a clean towel.

Use the tracing paper as a guide as you pin the work in place and leave it overnight to dry. Thread the pins though chain spaces and picot stitches where possible.

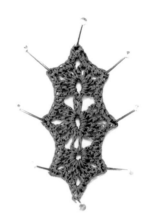

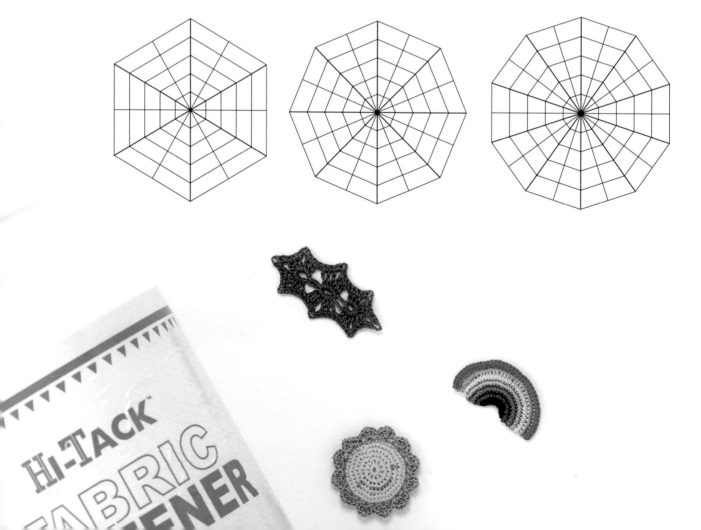

Stuffing

Toy stuffing

Light and fluffy toy stuffing is popular, but using it for small pieces can be a challenge as it is easy to tangle up your last rounds of crochet with those pesky fibres that love to poke through the opening of your amigurumi.

Yarn scraps

It's sustainable and free! I use this for most of my projects, as it is easier to stuff and trim some yarn than it is to battle with the fibres of toy stuffing.

Fabric bundles

This solves the fibre problem that you would get with toy stuffing and would be ideal for simple shapes like ball or oval shape amigurumi. It makes the overall piece firmer and adds extra weight, which is great for jewellery. Simply take a small square of fabric, wrap it tightly into your desired shape and bind it further by sewing and wrapping thread to make it is secure and compact. I recommend making one before you start to crochet so you can check for fit as you complete your project.

Reinforcements

Some 3D pieces when crocheted on a smaller scale need further reinforcement to maintain their shape. This is especially true for the geometric pieces such as the Amigurumi Cake Slice project in the Food chapter. Reinforcements can be made from card or foldable plastic like used stationary (think plastic binder or note pad covers) or clean food packaging. Simply trim and fold into shape and place into the inner walls of your crochet piece before stuffing.

Jewellery

Tools and materials

JUMP RINGS

These are the connectors that you can open and close with pliers to attach your crocheted pieces to other jewellery findings. They are mostly circular or oval shaped, come in different sizes and types of metal, and can be bought open or soldered closed.

SPLIT BAILS

These connect a pendant to a chain. Bails come in many shapes, sizes and mechanisms for different types of pendant, but a split bail is ideal because it can be opened to thread through crochet stitches.

CHAINS

There are many different types of chain, but the main things to look out for are the length and the quality of fastenings. Check the size of the fastenings to make sure that they are small enough to fit through your chosen pendant bail.

EAR WIRES

These are used for dangly drop earrings and come in different shapes and sizes. When shopping for ear wires, I look at the thickness of the wire, as thin ones can become misshapen. Sometimes I re-bend them with pliers to achieve a more desirable shape.

EAR BALL STUDS

These are a nice alternative to ear wires. They have a very small jump ring at the bottom that you can use to attach a crocheted item or another jump ring.

EAR DISC STUDS

These are common ear studs which are disc shaped.

EAR STUD BACKS

When choosing these remember that the larger and comfier they are the better.

BEADS

Round 2mm or seed beads are the best ones to use. Go for silver, glass, or whatever colours take your fancy.

HEAD PINS

These are available in different lengths, wire thicknesses, and head shapes. Have a look at the Mis-matched Planet Earrings project to see how these can be used.

JEWELLERY PLIERS

There are many types of pliers and each has its own function. Some have a silicone coating to prevent surface marking on the jewellery, some have a serrated surface for grip, but most have a flat steel surface. For most of the jewellery in this book, you will only need 1 to 2 pairs of needle-nose or flat-nose pliers with a flat surface for opening and closing jump rings. For incorporating wire-work into your crochet you will also need round-nose pliers and cutting pliers.

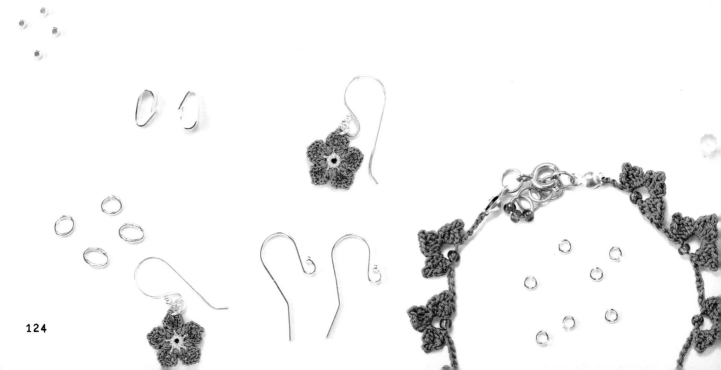

Jewellery techniques

OPENING JUMP RINGS

To open and close jump rings, use two pairs of pliers to hold the ring on either side of the split. Push one pair of pliers backwards and pull the other forwards, pushing the ends of the jump ring away from each other. This way they do not become misshapen when closing the jump ring.

ATTACHING JUMP RINGS

Where possible, attach a jump ring to either a chain space, a magic ring or a stitch below the last row or round of crochet. Use a fine crochet hook to prise a hole in the crochet work. Never attach it to the outer stitches as these are not strong enough and the cotton could snap.

MAKING PENDANTS

The jewellery finding used to attach pendants to chains are referred to as a bail, of which there are many different types. For crochet jewellery I tend to use split bails and heavy solid jump rings. More information can be found in the Flower Jewellery project in the Flowers chapter.

MAKING DANGLY EARRINGS

Two small jump rings are needed per earring so that it hangs and dangles nicely against the face. Jump rings in this case can also be attached via the magic ring if it is close to the edge of the crochet piece **(1)**.

MAKING EARRINGS WITH STUDS

For this you will need E6000 glue, a little sandpaper, small pieces of scrap paper, bulldog or binder clips and ear studs with a disc.

Abrade the surface of the disc with sandpaper and add a small amount of E6000 glue to the ear stud post. I like to spread it to the edges of the disc and leave the centre with no glue. This reduces the risk of the glue coming through a magic ring and being stuck to the ear stud post. Leave for a few minutes until it goes tacky and is close to solidifying, at this point you can attach the crochet motif and hold it in place with clips **(2)**.

Next, crochet a small disc in a matching colour, which is the same size as the disc on the ear stud post. Thread the ear stud through the magic ring of the crochet disc and sew it to the back of the ear stud **(3)**. This disguises any residual glue and guarantees that the flower won't come off.

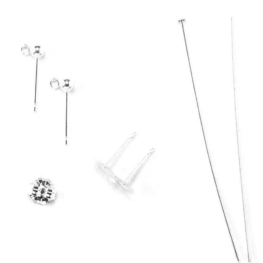

About the author

Steffi is a jewellery maker, crochet pattern designer and a design and technology secondary school teacher in North Yorkshire, England. She specialises in micro-crochet jewellery and draws inspiration from the natural world, vintage textile pieces and nostalgic crochet heirlooms such granny square blankets. She has a multi-disciplinary background in metal work, textiles, ceramics and laser cutting, having graduated in 2013 with a degree in Design Crafts from De Montfort University.

Suppliers

Duttons for Buttons for Gütermann threads, John James needles, jewellery findings and toy stuffing.

duttonsforbuttons.co.uk, 01904 632042

Gillies Fabrics for Gütermann threads.

gilliesfabrics.co.uk, 01904 626244

Wool Warehouse for Gütermann threads, DMC threads and crochet cotton, Ricorumi crochet cotton, Anchor threads, and Clover and Tulip crochet hooks.

woolwarehouse.co.uk

DMC for crochet yarn, embroidery threads and crochet threads sizes 10 to 80.

DMC.co.uk

Connecting Threads, America-based, for hand quilting cotton thread.

connectingthreads.com

Amazon shops for beads, jewellery pliers, toy stuffing, E6000 glue, pins, foam core board and liquid fabric solution for stiffening.

amazon.co.uk

The Bead Shop for jewellery supplies.

the-beadshop.co.uk

Beads Direct for jewellery supplies.

beadsdirect.co.uk

A very special thank you

To my family, Kate, Kirsty, Matthew, Jon, Mum and Dennis, Joanne, Cag and Mick, John and Irene.

To my friends, Kathryn, Martin, Issy, Kerry, Kim, Katy, Amy, Liz, John and Tanya and the ladies at Duttons. Your ability to encourage, reassure, tolerate and feed me is quite frankly a Herculean task and I don't know how you do it. Thank you for your unrelenting love and support, I love you all.

To everyone at David and Charles, your faith in me and my work has made the the process of writing my first book a pleasure, thank you so much.

Index

A DAVID AND CHARLES BOOK
© David and Charles, Ltd 2021

David and Charles is an imprint of David and Charles, Ltd, Suite A, Tourism House, Pynes Hill, Exeter, EX2 5WS

Text and Designs © Steffi Glaves 2021
Layout and Photography © David and Charles, Ltd 2021

First published in the UK and USA in 2021

Steffi Glaves has asserted her right to be identified as author of this work in accordance with the Copyright, Designs and Patents Act, 1988.

A catalogue record for this book is available from the British Library.

ISBN-13: 9781446308394 paperback
ISBN-13: 9781446379967 EPUB

This book has been printed on paper from approved suppliers and made from pulp from sustainable sources.

Printed in the UK by Pureprint for:
David and Charles, Ltd
Suite A, Tourism House, Pynes Hill, Exeter, EX2 5WS

10 9 8 7 6 5 4 3 2 1

Publishing Director: Ame Verso
Senior Commissioning Editor: Sarah Callard
Managing Editor: Jeni Chown
Editor: Jessica Cropper
Project Editor: Carol Ibbetson
Proofreader: Marie Clayton
Head of Design: Anna Wade
Senior Designer: Lucy Waldron
Pre-press Designer: Ali Stark
Illustrations: Kuo Kang Chen
Photography: Jason Jenkins
Production Manager: Beverley Richardson

David and Charles publishes high-quality books on a wide range of subjects. For more information visit www.davidandcharles.com.

Layout of the digital edition of this book may vary depending on reader hardware and display settings.